Learning Virtual Reality

Developing Immersive Experiences and
Applications for Desktop, Web, and Mobile

Tony Parisi

Beijing · Boston · Farnham · Sebastopol · Tokyo   O'REILLY®

Learning Virtual Reality

by Tony Parisi

Copyright © 2016 Tony Parisi. All rights reserved.

Printed in the United States of America.

Published by O'Reilly Media, Inc., 1005 Gravenstein Highway North, Sebastopol, CA 95472.

O'Reilly books may be purchased for educational, business, or sales promotional use. Online editions are also available for most titles (*http://safaribooksonline.com*). For more information, contact our corporate/institutional sales department: 800-998-9938 or *corporate@oreilly.com*.

Editors: Simon St.Laurent and Meg Foley	**Indexer:** Ellen Troutman-Zaig
Production Editor: Colleen Lobner	**Interior Designer:** David Futato
Copyeditor: Rachel Head	**Cover Designer:** Karen Montgomery
Proofreader: Charles Roumeliotis	**Illustrator:** Rebecca Demarest

November 2015:   First Edition

Revision History for the First Edition

2015-10-22:   First Release

See *http://oreilly.com/catalog/errata.csp?isbn=9781491922835* for release details.

978-1-491-92283-5

[LSI]

Table of Contents

Preface

Virtual reality has captured the world's imagination. Over the last few years, developers and enthusiasts in the thousands have devoted countless hours to coding, designing, and speculating about the possibilities of this exciting new medium. Affordable hardware systems like the *Oculus Rift*, *Samsung Gear VR*, and *Google Cardboard VR* allow consumers to experience virtual reality firsthand in the comfort of their homes, in a cafe, or on the train to work. Press coverage has reached beyond the trade press and blogosphere to mainstream publications extolling the virtues of VR, and the possibilities seem endless: from gaming and cinema to architecture, education, training, and medicine. Even though it has a long way to go, virtual reality appears poised to become the next major entertainment medium, and perhaps even the computing platform of the future.

I first tried an Oculus Rift in the summer of 2013. I was, to put it bluntly, underwhelmed. The graphics of the original development kit (the so-called "DK1") were low-res by today's standards, and I lasted about 10 minutes before the nausea kicked in—which, according to my friend Dave, was an impressive display of endurance. I put the device aside, grumbled "not ready," staggered back to work, and didn't give the matter much thought again until nine months later, when the tech industry was set on its ear by the announcement that social media giant Facebook had acquired Oculus VR, the makers of the Rift. Like many of my peers, I was stunned. Also, like many of my peers, I decided to jump right in and start developing something in VR.

Since the watershed Oculus acquisition, the industry has invested millions in developing applications, content, tools, display hardware, video capture systems, and peripherals. Big tech players are already staking out their turf, making bets on what the future will look like with respect to distribution channels, "killer apps," and such, and creating platforms and ecosystems to align with their visions. Developers of all shapes and sizes are flocking to VR, some out of genuine excitement for a new medium with great potential, and others preparing to take advantage of what could be the next tech boom after mobile. However it all ultimately shakes out, being a VR developer promises to be an exciting ride.

Every journey begins with a first step, and this book is here to set you on your path. It's not deep; the goal is to familiarize you with core programming concepts, and the innovations in hardware and software that have made VR possible. It *is* broad: we cover three of the major platforms, using three different development environments and as many programming languages. By the end, you should come away with the feeling that you understand the basics, and a desire to learn more.

Audience

This book was written for programmers and designers looking for an introduction to virtual reality development. It assumes at least entry-level programming experience, but you don't have to be a professional developer to read it. Creative coders, producers with a programming background, and technically savvy artists should also be able to follow along. I want anyone who likes to make things on a computer to be able to walk away having learned something from this book.

Readers should know the basics of JavaScript, Java, C#, or another C-family programming language. Experience with 3D graphics is also helpful. If you don't have 3D experience, Chapter 3 contains a primer that you may find useful.

If you are a professional developer, a lot of this material will seem basic to you. But go through it carefully: interleaved with the how-tos and 101s are essential nuggets of technical information for putting together desktop, mobile, and web VR apps. It represents many hours of carefully working through the details of various tools, SDKs, APIs, and operating systems, including suffering through a few major upgrades that were sprung on me halfway through writing the manuscript. Maybe my effort will help save you from hitting those same land mines along the way.

If you are a native developer of mobile and desktop apps, and know Unity3D or another game engine, then this book should help you extend your skills into VR. If you are comfortable developing for WebGL, then you should have an easy time creating VR for the Web with the introduction of just a few new concepts. If you are a newbie at both, no worries; I like to think I wrote the book in a way that will get you going, no matter your starting point.

How This Book Is Organized

This book is divided into seven chapters, as follows:

- Chapters 1 and 2 provide an introduction to virtual reality concepts and survey the new hardware systems coming to market.
- Chapters 3 through 6 cover virtual reality development in detail. This is the heart of the book, in which we look at developing for three of the major virtual reality hardware systems: the Oculus Rift, Gear VR, and Cardboard VR. These chapters

explore different tools for creating VR applications, including Unity3D and Android Studio, as well as several programming languages. There is also a chapter about creating web-based VR applications using WebVR, a new JavaScript API supported in development versions of popular browsers like Firefox and Chrome.

- Chapter 7 brings the concepts introduced in Chapters 3 through 6 together in a simple working application: a 360-degree panoramic VR photo viewer for Google Cardboard, built in Unity3D.

Conventions Used in This Book

The following typographical conventions are used in this book:

Italic
Indicates new terms, URLs, email addresses, filenames, and file extensions.

`Constant width`
Used for program listings, as well as within paragraphs to refer to program elements such as variable or function names, databases, objects, parameters, and values.

`Constant width bold`
Shows commands or other text that should be typed literally by the user.

`Constant width italic`
Shows text that should be replaced with user-supplied values or by values determined by context.

 This element signifies a general note.

Using Code Examples

Supplemental material for this book is available for download at *https://github.com/ tparisi/LearningVirtualReality* and *https://github.com/tparisi/WebVR*.

This book is here to help you get your job done. In general, if example code is offered with this book, you may use it in your programs and documentation. You do not need to contact us for permission unless you're reproducing a significant portion of the code. For example, writing a program that uses several chunks of code from this book does not require permission. Selling or distributing a CD-ROM of examples from O'Reilly books does require permission. Answering a question by citing this book and quoting example code does not require permission. Incorporating a significant amount of example code from this book into your product's documentation does require permission.

We appreciate, but do not require, attribution. An attribution usually includes the title, author, publisher, and ISBN. For example: "*Learning Virtual Reality* by Tony Parisi (O'Reilly). Copyright 2016 Tony Parisi, 978-1-4919-2283-5."

If you feel your use of code examples falls outside fair use or the permission given above, feel free to contact us at *permissions@oreilly.com*.

About Third-Party Copyrighted Material

Note that some of the content assets used in this book are subject to copyright. Their creators have kindly granted me permission to redistribute them for use with the book for the *sole* purpose of supporting the programming examples included. For any other purpose, including and especially use in your applications, you must obtain your own copies of those assets, which may include purchasing a license.

Safari® Books Online

 Safari Books Online is an on-demand digital library that delivers expert content in both book and video form from the world's leading authors in technology and business.

Technology professionals, software developers, web designers, and business and creative professionals use Safari Books Online as their primary resource for research, problem solving, learning, and certification training.

Safari Books Online offers a range of plans and pricing for enterprise, government, education, and individuals.

Members have access to thousands of books, training videos, and prepublication manuscripts in one fully searchable database from publishers like O'Reilly Media, Prentice Hall Professional, Addison-Wesley Professional, Microsoft Press, Sams, Que, Peachpit Press, Focal Press, Cisco Press, John Wiley & Sons, Syngress, Morgan Kaufmann, IBM Redbooks, Packt, Adobe Press, FT Press, Apress, Manning, New Riders, McGraw-Hill, Jones & Bartlett, Course Technology, and hundreds more. For more information about Safari Books Online, please visit us online.

How to Contact Us

Please address comments and questions concerning this book to the publisher:

O'Reilly Media, Inc.
1005 Gravenstein Highway North
Sebastopol, CA 95472
800-998-9938 (in the United States or Canada)
707-829-0515 (international or local)
707-829-0104 (fax)

We have a web page for this book, where we list errata, examples, and any additional information. You can access this page at *http://bit.ly/learning-virtual-reality*.

To comment or ask technical questions about this book, send email to *bookquestions@oreilly.com*.

For more information about our books, courses, conferences, and news, see our website at *http://www.oreilly.com*.

Find us on Facebook: *http://facebook.com/oreilly*

Follow us on Twitter: *http://twitter.com/oreillymedia*

Watch us on YouTube: *http://www.youtube.com/oreillymedia*

Acknowledgments

It takes a village to make a good VR book, and I was able to lean on some great developers to get my job done. "That VR Guy" Dave Arendash and Alex Sink of RIVER Studios provided much-needed expert information on using Unity3D. Patrick Chen and Andrew Dickerson from Samsung lent early moral support (and a Gear VR) to get me going with mobile development. The WebVR brain trust, including Josh Carpenter, Vlad Vukićević, Diego Marcos, and Brandon Jones, have been stalwart, always ready with advice and answers to questions, and always willing to consider an API design change.

I am grateful for the excellent technical reviews done for the book, especially the review by my friend and startup collaborator Jason Marsh. Jason worked through the code examples in painstaking detail, and identified several critical issues. Jason also contributed the beautiful panoramic photos featured in the example in Chapter 7.

I would like to thank the team at O'Reilly, especially my editor, Meg Foley. Meg was exceedingly patient with my halting progress due to conflicting startup commitments. She also gave me much-needed encouragement when I hit a snag and had to rewrite several chapters due to massive changes in the Oculus SDK software. That's life on the bleeding edge, I guess, but nevertheless, Meg has been a champ.

Finally, thanks to my family. Marina and Lucian are used to my book-writing antics by now, but each one is a new exercise in forbearance. Guys, you're the best.

CHAPTER 1

Introduction

Virtual reality is a medium with tremendous potential. The ability to be transported to other places, to be fully immersed in experiences, and to feel like you're really there—*present*—opens up previously unimagined ways to interact and communicate. Until recently, virtual reality was out of reach for the average consumer due to cost and other factors. However, advances in the technology over the last few years have set the stage for a mass-market revolution that could be as influential as the introduction of television, the Internet, or the smartphone.

Virtual reality—VR for short—comprises a collection of technologies: 3D displays, motion tracking hardware, input devices, software frameworks, and development tools. While consumer-grade VR hardware is young and evolving, a handful of platforms have emerged as go-to choices, including the Oculus Rift, Samsung Gear VR, and Google Cardboard. Each delivers a different level of VR experience, at a different price point, with varying degrees of in-your-hands portability.

Software to create and display consumer virtual reality is also coming together rapidly. The Unity3D and Unreal game engines, popular for making desktop and mobile games, have become tools of choice for native VR development. And the Web is not far behind: WebGL and 3D JavaScript frameworks like Three.js and Babylon.js are providing a path for creating open source, browser-based virtual reality experiences for desktop and mobile operating systems.

It's an exciting time! With so much energy going into development, and so much consumer interest, VR just might be the next big wave of computer technology. In this book, we explore the hardware, software, application techniques, and interface design challenges encountered by today's virtual reality creator. Virtual reality is still in its early stages. It's a lot like the Wild West, and you are a pioneer. The landscape may be fraught with unknowns, even dangers—but we push on, driven by the promise of a better life. Let's take a peek at this new frontier.

Figure 1-1 shows a screenshot of the now-famous Tuscany VR demo, created by the team at Oculus VR to show off their hardware. Put on the Oculus Rift and launch the demo. You are on the grounds of a Tuscan estate, looking at a beautiful villa. Clouds drift lazily across the sky. You hear birds chirping, and the sound of waves lapping gently against a shore.

You move through the scene, video game–style, using the W, A, S, and D keys on your keyboard (known to gamers as the "WASD keys"). If you play a lot of PC games, this is nothing new. But now, turn your head: looking up, down, and behind, you can see the entire estate. You are there, immersed in a virtual world that completely surrounds you. Walk forward, into the villa, and take a look around. Walk out, up to the edge of the property, and see the lake below. For a few moments at least, you forget that you are not actually in this other place. You're *present*.

This feeling of total immersion—of being somewhere else, experiencing something else entirely—is what we are striving for with virtual reality. And this is where our journey begins.

Figure 1-1. Tuscany VR demo by the Oculus VR team

What Is Virtual Reality?

> *Reality is merely an illusion, albeit a very persistent one.*
> —Albert Einstein

Virtual reality has one goal: to convince you that you are somewhere else. It does this by tricking the human brain—in particular, the visual cortex and parts of the brain that perceive motion. A variety of technologies conspire to create this illusion, including:

Stereoscopic displays
> Also known as *3D displays* or *head-mounted displays* (HMDs), these displays use a combination of multiple images, realistic optical distortion, and special lenses to produce a stereo image that our eyes interpret as having three-dimensional depth.

Motion tracking hardware
> Gyroscopes, accelerometers, and other low-cost components are used in virtual reality hardware to sense when our bodies move and our heads turn, so that the application can update our view into the 3D scene.

Input devices
> Virtual reality is creating the need for new types of input devices beyond the keyboard and mouse, including game controllers and hand- and body-tracking sensors that can recognize motion and gestures.

Desktop and mobile platforms
> This includes the computer hardware, operating systems, software to interface to the devices, frameworks and engines that run applications, and software tools for building them.

Without all four of these components, it is hard to achieve a fully immersive virtual reality experience. We will dive further into the details throughout the book; for now, let's take a quick look at each.

Stereoscopic Displays

The main ingredient in virtual reality is a persistent 3D visual representation of the experience that conveys a sense of depth. To create this depth, virtual reality hardware systems employ a 3D display, also known as a stereoscopic display or head-mounted display.

For years, one of the biggest impediments to consumer-grade virtual reality was an affordable stereoscopic display that is light and comfortable enough to be worn for an extended period. This situation changed dramatically when the team from Oculus VR created the Oculus Rift. First introduced in 2012, the Rift was a breakthrough in VR hardware, featuring a stereoscopic display and a head-tracking sensor built into a lightweight headset that could be purchased as a development kit for a few hundred dollars. While the original development kit, known as the DK1, was fairly low-resolution, it was enough to get the entire industry excited and unleash a storm of VR development. Newer Rift development kit versions, such as the DK2 depicted in Figure 1-2, feature higher display resolution, position as well as orientation tracking, and better performance.

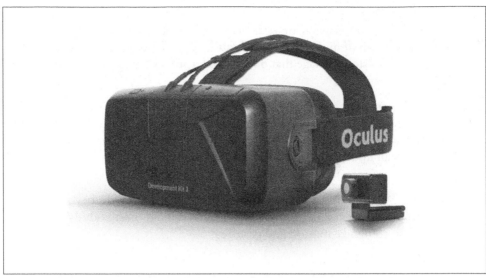

Figure 1-2. The Oculus Rift head-mounted display, Development Kit 2

So what does the Oculus Rift actually do? To create the illusion of depth, we need to generate a separate image for each eye, one slightly offset from the other, to simulate *parallax*—the visual phenomenon where our brains perceive depth based on the difference in the apparent position of objects (due to our eyes being slightly apart from each other). To create a really good illusion, we also want to distort the image to better emulate the spherical shape of the eye, using a technique known as *barrel distortion*. The Oculus Rift does both.

A more accurate screenshot of the Tuscany VR demo, a capture of the entire display that renders this scene in virtual reality using these two techniques, would look like Figure 1-3. This shows the rendering as it appears on a computer screen connected to the Oculus Rift's head-mounted display.

From a software point of view, an Oculus Rift application's job is to render an image like the one in Figure 1-3 a minimum of 60 and ideally 120 times per second, to avoid any perceived lag, or *latency*, that might break the illusion or, worse, lead to the nausea that is often associated with poorly performing VR. Exactly how we do this in our applications is the subject of another chapter.

Note that the Oculus Rift is not the only game in town. As we will see in the next chapter, there are several head-mounted displays to choose from. Some of these work only with desktop computers, others are just for smartphones, and still others can only be used with game consoles. The HMDs come in a variety of styles and a range of prices. But as consumer-ready virtual reality displays go, Oculus is the first and—as of this writing—still the best.

Figure 1-3. Tuscany VR demo rendered in stereo for the Oculus Rift

Motion Tracking Hardware

The second essential trick for making the brain believe it is in another place is to track movements of the head and update the rendered scene in real time. This mimics what happens when we look around in the real world.

One of the innovations in the Oculus Rift is its rapid head motion tracking using a high-speed *inertial measurement unit* (IMU). Head-tracking IMUs combine gyroscope, accelerometer, and/or magnetometer hardware, similar to that found in smartphones today, to precisely measure changes in rotation. The VR hardware systems covered in the next chapter employ a variety of IMU configurations.

Motion tracking of the head is as important as quality stereo rendering, if not more so. Our perceptual systems are very sensitive to motion, and like lag in stereo rendering, high latency in head tracking can break the feeling of immersion and/or cause nausea. Virtual reality IMU hardware must track head movement as rapidly as possible, and the software must keep up. When stereo rendering and head motion tracking are properly combined, and updated with enough frequency, we can achieve a true feeling of being immersed in the experience.

Input Devices

To create a convincing feeling of immersion, head-mounted displays completely enclose the user's eyes, cutting them off from seeing the outside world. This makes for an interesting situation with respect to input: users have to "fly blind"; they cannot see their mouse or keyboard when using the VR display. To address this, VR is making use of alternate types of input devices, including game controllers, hand-tracking motion sensors, and wireless hand and body trackers.

There is currently no one standard way to interact, no "mouse of virtual reality," if you will. VR is driving a lot of experimentation and innovation with respect to input devices, and we are only at the beginning of that process. Over the next few years, we may see a complete transformation of how we interact with our computers, thanks to VR.

Computing Platforms

Many VR applications will run on a majority of existing computers and mobile phones. A relatively modern desktop or high-powered laptop can do the trick with Oculus Rift; smartphones can also offer a good VR experience, provided they have enough CPU and graphics power. For most of us, this means that our existing computers and devices can be turned into virtual reality boxes simply by adding a few peripherals. But for those seeking super high production value experiences, the latest desktop PC with a best-of-breed graphics processor and the fastest available CPU might be the top item on the wish list for next Christmas.

As VR matures and gains in popularity, we may also begin to see dedicated computers, phones, and consoles—dedicated, that is, to the sole purpose of enabling amazing virtual reality.

Software to create VR applications comes in several flavors: native software development kits, game engines and frameworks, and even the latest versions of modern web browsers. VR video is another area of exploration. Let's take a closer look at each of these development options.

Native software development kits (SDKs)

These are the device drivers and software libraries used in conjunction with the computer's host operating system. On Windows they would be Win32 libraries used in C++ applications; on Android, they would be Java libraries; and so on. You can build a native application simply using the SDKs, and "roll your own" with respect to everything else (such as 3D graphics and game behaviors). But most developers use engines or frameworks.

Game engines and frameworks

Unless you are a game engine developer, you probably won't want to deal with the native SDKs directly; you will more than likely turn to a game engine such as Unity3D (described in detail in Chapter 3). Libraries like Unity3D, also known as *middleware*, take care of the low-level details of 3D rendering, physics, game behaviors, and interfacing to devices. Most VR developers today build their apps using game middleware like Unity3D.

Many middleware engines have strong cross-platform support, allowing you to write your code once (most of it, at least) and target multiple platforms, including desktop and mobile. They also usually come with a powerful set of tools known as *level editors* or *integrated development environments* (IDEs).

Web browsers

Much in the way that HTML5 added mobile features over a short number of years, nearly achieving parity with native mobile capability, browser makers are fast following the development of virtual reality. In the case of VR, the adoption of features into web browsers is looking like it will only take one or two years, not four to five.

The upshot of this is twofold: first, it means that we can use web technologies like HTML5, WebGL, and JavaScript to create our applications, making it potentially faster to code and more cross-platform; second, it affords us access to all of the existing infrastructure the Web has to offer, such as hyperlinking between VR experiences, hosting content in the cloud, developing multiuser shared experiences, and integrating web data directly into our virtual reality applications.

Video players

Stereoscopic video represents a whole class of virtual reality technology by itself. Unlike with game engines, where the application's graphics are completely synthetic, based on handcrafted 3D models, animations, backgrounds, and so on, stereo video is captured from the real world. This makes for truly realistic and often stunning experiences: imagine taking a virtual helicopter tour of the Grand Canyon in VR, being able to look around as you fly over the canyon. Video is not fully interactive in the way that a 3D virtual environment can be though, so the use of this media type has some limitations.

Stereo video recording requires multiple cameras. The minimum is two, but if we want the video to be *panoramic*—that is, capture a 360-degree view of an entire scene for use in virtual reality—then we need even more cameras. Pioneers in the field, such as California-based Jaunt VR, are experimenting with setups that use dozens of cameras to make the first VR feature-length films.

The capture and production of VR video is a nascent field. Several companies and research projects are devoting their efforts to it. There are also a variety of VR video players in development. Some players work only in native environments, while others are only for mobile or the Web, but some developers are creating full cross-platform players. One of the biggest issues in this young endeavor is that there are as yet no standard formats for storing and playing back of the videos, so if you want to produce video content, you may have to choose a single vendor for the hardware, the production tools, and the playback software.

Virtual Reality Applications

Even though consumer virtual reality is just a few years old, we are already seeing a staggering range of applications. To say that VR has captured people's imaginations would be an understatement. Developers are trying to build virtually *everything* in VR, understandably with mixed success so far.

While it is way too early to pick winners and identify "killer apps" for VR, there are several domains that show great promise, including:

Video games
> This is an obvious candidate, the one that most people immediately imagine when you tell them about virtual reality. The potential for deep immersion, higher production value, and stickier engagement has developers, console makers, and peripheral manufacturers salivating in anticipation. It is fair to assume that the majority of skilled, independent, large development shops creating VR are currently doing so for games.

Virtual worlds
> Social, user-generated persistent virtual worlds could be a powerful combination with virtual reality immersion. Companies like High Fidelity, created by *Second Life* founder Philip Rosedale, and AltSpace VR, a new San Francisco Bay Area startup, are leading this charge.

Education
> For years, 3D visualization has been a great tool for interactive learning; VR immersion could make learning even more approachable and effective.

Productivity
> Some researchers and small companies are exploring using VR as a replacement for the decades-old desktop computer metaphor. Imagine a virtual reality, 360-degree workspace that holds your personal information, contacts, work projects, etc.

Tourism
> Stereoscopic 360-degree panoramas in VR are really compelling. They represent a simple, effective way to convey the experience of being elsewhere without having to get on a plane.

Architecture and real estate
> Architecture and real estate firms are already experimenting with virtual reality, using both video and interactive graphics. Video can be great for showing existing properties; interactive graphics work well for visualization of buildings and complexes in the planning stages (i.e., using 3D CAD models).

Live events

VR video is promising to be quite popular for concerts, news reporting, and other live events. Musicians Paul McCartney and Jack White are among several rock stars who have already broadcast virtual reality versions of their live shows.

Web browsing

Mozilla is leading the charge in experimenting with adding VR support to its browser, and Google is not far behind in creating the same features for Chrome. Beyond building the technology plumbing, the research team at Mozilla is exploring visual and interface designs for how to navigate a universe of information in virtual reality.

Enterprise applications

There are countless potential VR applications for the enterprise, including simulation and training for military use, medical diagnostics and training, and engineering and design.

This list is just a sampling. We have no way of knowing which applications will be most successful in a new medium like virtual reality, or what will become popular. We also can't predict what other ideas will spring from the minds of clever folks—but if the last few decades of technology have taught us anything, it's that whatever people come up with, it will probably be something we never could have imagined before.

Chapter Summary

Consumer virtual reality is upon us. As we have seen in this chapter, VR brings together several technologies, including 3D stereoscopic displays, motion tracking hardware, new input devices, computers, and mobile phones. The key innovations that enable virtual reality are stereoscopic rendering and motion tracking. When these two are properly combined, we feel immersed, or *present*, and the illusion of VR is compelling enough to transport us to another place.

There are a variety of development options for virtual reality: native SDKs that access raw platform features; game engines that give us more power and cross-platform reach; web browsers, for creating shared, connected virtual reality apps; and video players and tools for creating stereoscopic panoramic videos based on the real world.

Though the technology is still immature, virtual reality is already being used in a number of applications, from games to education, from real estate to rock concerts. Developers are also creating productivity and enterprise applications, looking to the power of VR immersion to enhance business value.

In the next chapter we will explore the wide variety of virtual reality hardware systems in use today. Let's get to it.

CHAPTER 2

Virtual Reality Hardware

In this chapter we will take a look at popular consumer virtual reality hardware in use today, including VR headsets and the computers or phones they work with.

Even though this is a rapidly evolving industry, some manufacturers are already becoming established as leaders. Most notable is Facebook with the Oculus Rift, but there are several other head-mounted displays (HMDs) to choose from. Some HMDs require using desktop computers, others are just for smartphones, and still others are for use with game consoles. To further muddy the picture, new HMDs are coming out all the time.

Let's examine three headsets that represent a wide range of HMDs on the market today, and that will form the focus of the rest of the chapters in the book: the Oculus Rift for desktop virtual reality; Samsung's Gear VR (based on Oculus technology) for a high-end mobile VR experience; and Google's Cardboard VR, a simple, low-cost way of adapting your existing smartphone to become a VR device.

Oculus Rift

While there have been several attempts to market consumer virtual reality headsets over the past few decades, nothing ever pushed it over the top until the Oculus Rift came along. Buoyed by an extremely successful Kickstarter campaign to fund its original development, Oculus VR raised significant venture funding, and the company was ultimately sold to Facebook in a blockbuster US$2B acquisition that the industry is still talking about. Without that watershed event, it is unlikely that virtual reality would have gotten as popular as quickly, or captured the public's interest in the way it has. But it did, and it has, and here we are.

The Oculus Rift has spawned an entire VR industry. This includes companies large and small creating applications, tools, peripheral hardware, and development services. Numerous applications are being built for the Oculus Rift, spanning gaming, architecture, medicine, real estate, tourism, entertainment, and education. With its voracious appetite for CPU and graphics processor cycles, the Rift has even given a shot in the arm to the declining desktop PC industry.

The Oculus Rift is a stereoscopic display with built-in head motion tracking sensors. It straps to the head, allowing hands-free operation. The Rift is a peripheral that attaches to a computer: Mac, Linux, or Windows (desktop or laptop). The Rift is tethered, with a cable running to the computer. At the moment it is quite bulky—but that will most certainly change with the newer models being designed as we speak.

The following is a brief history of the Oculus Rift, by way of exploring the evolution of this groundbreaking VR headset.

The Gold Standard of Virtual Reality

By any reckoning, as of this writing the Oculus Rift i s applications, the virtual reality headset against which all others will be measured in coming years. While the current development kit versions still feel clunky in some ways, each iteration is noticeably better than the last. Oculus VR has publicly announced plans for a retail consumer headset release in early 2016 that promises to be affordable, comfortable, and amazing.

The DK1

The original Oculus Rift development kit, known as the *DK1*, is a big affair—weighing in at over 13 ounces (.33 kg) and measuring 7 inches (18 cm) diagonal—and therefore not very comfortable for extended use. It has an external control box in addition to two sets of wires: one for the USB connection to the head tracker, and one for the video signal coming from the computer. The DK1 is depicted in Figure 2-1.

The DK1 has a resolution of 1280x800 pixels. This screen real estate is divided between the two eyes, so the effective resolution is 640x800; in other words, the DK1 is a low-resolution device by today's standards for computer monitors. The display has a horizontal field of view of well over 90 degrees, which is important for emulating the visual field of view experienced in the real world. The head tracking of the inertial measurement unit (IMU) is quite fast at 250 Hz; this is critical to enable a true sense of immersion and to reduce motion sickness.

Despite its low visual resolution, the wide field of view and rapid head tracking response time of the DK1 made it the first practical low-cost VR headset, at least for short sessions. And it was promising enough to get Oculus VR off the ground as a company. Oculus initially made DK1 units available to its Kickstarter backers in the summer of 2012, then sold them online to the general public in late 2012. Then, infused with a large round of venture capital, the company went straight to work on the next generation, the DK2.

Figure 2-1. The original Oculus development kit, or DK1

The DK2

In the spring of 2014, Oculus released the second major incarnation of its headset. In contrast with the unwieldy DK1, the Oculus Rift DK2 is a sleek device. It is still quite large, covering a good portion of the user's face, but it is much lighter and features a more pleasing form factor than its predecessor. It also has only one cable coming out of the HMD, which then splits into the HDMI and USB cables that connect to the computer's video and USB ports, respectively.

The DK2 improved upon its predecessor with a lower-persistence, 1920x1080 display (960x1080 per eye). Beyond the display improvements, the DK2 incorporated a major advancement: positional head tracking. This allows the user to not only look around, but move around within a virtual scene—forward, back, side to side, and up and down. However, use of the positional tracker requires being in front of a tracking camera mounted on the computer, which effectively means the user needs to stay within a small zone near the computer. The positional tracking also only works when the user is facing the camera.

The DK2 was depicted in Figure 1-2 (see Chapter 1). The tracking camera for the DK2 is pictured in Figure 2-2.

Figure 2-2. Positional tracking camera for the Oculus Rift DK2

DK2 and the Examples in This Book

As of this writing, the DK2 is the primary Oculus Rift device being used in development. The examples throughout the book have been developed for the DK2, using the associated software development kit (SDK).

Crescent Bay

The third major Oculus Rift developer version is code-named *Crescent Bay*. Crescent Bay features greater capabilities and big improvements in design. It has a higher resolution display and 360-degree head tracking, meaning that you don't have to be looking at the tracking camera; there are position sensors mounted at the rear of the device as well. Crescent Bay is depicted in Figure 2-3.

As of this writing, Crescent Bay is only available as a demo. It is presumed that it, or a model quite close to it, will ship as a development kit version sometime in 2015, in preparation for the release of the first Oculus retail headset (known as "CV1" for Consumer Version 1) in early 2016. Great content has already been created for this third development kit version, including *Senza Peso* (*http://bit.ly/senza-peso*), the cinematic experience shown in Figure 2-4. *Senza Peso* is a companion piece to the short film/opera of the same name: it is an innovative, expressionistic exploration of the afterlife that was created by Los Angeles–based studio Kite and Lightning.

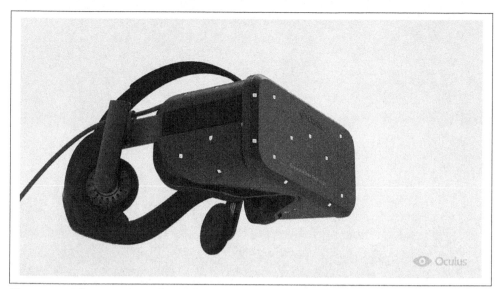

Figure 2-3. The newest Oculus Rift, code-named "Crescent Bay"

Really Real Virtual Reality

Anyone who has been privileged to try a demo of Crescent Bay will attest that it represents a major leap in capability over the DK2. In my opinion, Crescent Bay is the difference between experiencing the *promise* of virtual reality and actually experiencing it. The level of realism and feeling of presence while in the demos is unmatched. There were many moments when I completely forgot that I was in a simulation... which I believe is the entire point. To cut a long story short: if you're ever offered a chance to check it out, don't pass it up.

As you can see, Oculus VR is continually striving to improve on its creation. The three major development kits each represent a big step forward in features and comfort. If this trajectory continues, then something truly astounding is in store for us when the company ships its first commercial version.

Setting Up Your Oculus Rift

If you are ready to take the plunge and buy a DK2, go to the Oculus Products tab and select DK2 (*http://bit.ly/oculus-rift-dk2*) to order it online. A few tips on getting started follow.

Figure 2-4. Senza Peso, a cinematic VR experience by Kite and Lightning

What Computer Do I Need?

To have the best experience with the Oculus Rift, you will want to connect it to a powerful desktop computer or laptop. As of this writing, Oculus is only actively supporting its SDK for developing on Windows. You can still find applications written for the Mac and Linux, and early SDK versions available for download on the Oculus developer site if you hunt for them. But for now, PCs are your best bet.

See the Oculus blog (*http://bit.ly/oculus-rec-spec*) for the team's recommended minimum system requirements for machines to run VR on the DK2 and newer models.

Downloading the Oculus runtime, examples, and SDK

The Oculus Rift is not yet a consumer product: setting up the hardware and software can be tricky and requires a modicum of technical knowledge and a lot of patience. In order to experience content using the Rift, you must at a minimum download the Oculus runtime for your platform. The runtime provides the software necessary for the Rift to communicate with your computer's operating system.

Oculus runtime installers can be found on the Oculus developer site (*https://developer.oculus.com/*). Once you have the runtime installed, you can try out the Oculus Rift by downloading and installing applications from a variety of sources (Appendix A contains a list of several sites that feature Oculus content). To get started, try out the official portal from Oculus, *Oculus Share (https://share.oculus.com/)*.

If you also wish to develop for the Oculus Rift, you will need to become an Oculus Developer and download the software development kit. If you don't have one already, go to the Oculus developer site to sign up for a free developer account. Then, log in and follow the instructions for your particular platform. Once you are set up with the SDK, you can develop desktop Oculus applications as described in Chapters 3 through 5.

Other High-End Head-Mounted Displays

The popularity of the Oculus Rift has led to a proliferation of head-mounted displays from different manufacturers. The following is a list of the more notable ones:

HTC Vive (http://www.htcvr.com/)
> The result of a partnership between hardware manufacturer HTC and gaming titan Valve (the makers of the *Steam* downloadable game service), the Vive represents another major step forward in virtual reality systems. It features a comfortable, high-resolution HMD, a 15x15-foot room-sized positional tracking system, and two ergonomically designed motion-sensing hand controllers for input.

OSVR (http://www.osvr.org/)
> Open Source Virtual Reality (OSVR) is an open specification for software and hardware devices supported through a collaboration of several companies, including long-time VR developer Sensics and peripherals maker Razer. OSVR is an ecosystem with which device manufacturers can build headsets and input devices that work interoperably, and developers can build applications using common APIs, without knowing the specifics of the underlying hardware. The Razer OSVR headset is depicted in Figure 2-5.

FOVE (http://www.getfove.com/)
> FOVE is the next generation of HMD, able to track not only head movements but *eye movements*, opening up whole new possibilities for VR applications.

Project Morpheus (http://bit.ly/proj-morph)
> Sony has created a virtual reality system for use with its PlayStation 4 console. The Morpheus features a comfortable HMD and two motion-sensing hand controllers for input.

Unfortunately for us as developers, none of these systems are compatible. Each requires custom programming using a different SDK. OSVR is attempting to provide an open, vendor-neutral way to talk to VR hardware, and this is promising; however, the software is too early in its adoption cycle to know whether it will become a standard API for programming VR.

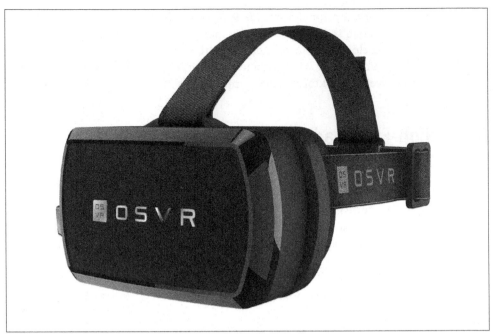

Figure 2-5. Razer's headset, based on the OSVR open specification

That's how it goes on the bleeding edge of technology. While we may someday see a universally adopted software stack for creating VR, for the foreseeable future we will have to choose among several conflicting options.

Samsung Gear VR: Deluxe, Portable Virtual Reality

The Oculus Rift may be the flagship VR headset, but it is not without its issues. First, it requires a very powerful computer with a fast graphics processor. If you try to run Rift applications with a garden-variety PC laptop, MacBook Air, or older desktop computer, you won't have much fun. The frame rate will be slow, which is not only dissatisfying but can actually produce nausea. Second, the Rift is bulky and connected to the computer with a wire. If you want to run applications that use DK2 positional tracking, you will need to install the position tracking camera that is shipped with the DK2 and sit yourself down right in front of it for the tracking to work. Finally, it is not very mobile. Yes, you can pack up a six-pound laptop and your Rift to take to a demo party, but it's not the kind of thing you will want to bring to Starbucks (believe me, I've seen it done and it's not pretty), or on your train commute. This all makes for a cumbersome, stationary experience—and a potentially expensive one if you also need to buy a new computer.

Anticipating these issues, Oculus has also produced a much more lightweight mobile solution. Through a partnership with Samsung, Oculus technology has been incorporated into the *Gear VR*, a revolutionary headset that combines Oculus optics (those barrel distortion lenses) with new head-tracking technology, placed in a custom headset that houses a mobile phone with a high-resolution display.

Samsung released the Gear VR as an "Innovator Edition" in late 2014. The Gear VR unit costs US$99 and can be purchased through Samsung's online store. It currently only works with the Samsung Galaxy Note 4 and S6 phones, so if you don't already own one of these phones, this can be a pricey option. But it is very high quality, and may be the killer mobile option for the next few years. The original Gear VR Innovator Edition is depicted in Figure 2-6.

Figure 2-6. The Samsung Gear VR

The Gear VR's graphics are stunning, thanks to the Samsung phones' display resolution of 2560x1440 pixels (1280x1440 per eye). The headset contains a custom IMU based on Oculus technology. The Gear VR IMU tracks much faster and with less latency (delay) than the IMU built into the phone itself.

The Gear VR housing has several intuitive input controls, including an eye adjustment wheel (for matching the device's interpupillary distance to your own), as well as controls that let you access functions of the phone within: a volume control, a headphone jack, and, most importantly, a trackpad for touch input.

The Gear VR is a fantastic consumer VR headset. A quick trip through the available demos and apps might even convince you that it's the best one on the market today. It offers a better experience than the DK2, with a much nicer form factor and amazing display resolution. If money were no object, this could be it—however, including a newly purchased phone, the price may be prohibitive for some. Of course, this situation could change if Samsung can figure out how to accommodate other phones, drop the total cost of ownership, or otherwise change the equation.

The Oculus Mobile SDK

Developing applications for the Gear VR's Android-based operating system requires a different Oculus SDK, called the Mobile SDK, which is also available on the Oculus developer website (*https://developer.oculus.com/*).

We will cover the basics of Gear VR development in Chapter 4.

Google Cardboard: Low-Cost VR for Smartphones

If they were automobiles, the Oculus Rift and Gear VR would be the Tesla and Lamborghini of VR headsets: best-of-breed but out of reach for the average consumer. The rough user experience, aggressive machine specs, and price tag in the hundreds of dollars mean that using a Rift is a major commitment. The Gear VR provides a sublime experience, but for now it is priced out of reach for anyone but a serious enthusiast or early adopter. Over time, the hope is that these higher-end consumer VR systems will become more affordable and accessible, and truly mass-consumer.

In the meantime, there is Google's *Cardboard VR*: a simple, low-cost way of adapting your existing smartphone to become a VR device. In 2014 Google introduced Cardboard VR, which allows users to experience virtual reality using pretty much any mobile phone, without the need for expensive additional hardware.

Google's original Cardboard VR unit, which debuted at the I/O conference in May 2014, is pictured in Figure 2-7.

To experience Cardboard VR, simply launch a Cardboard-ready application and place your mobile phone into the box. You will be immersed in a VR experience: a stereo-rendered 3D scene that you can look around and move around in by turning your head. Not bad for two bucks!

Cardboard is actually a reference specification. Google doesn't offer it as a product; you can get the specifications (*http://bit.ly/manufacture-cardboard*) from them and build one of your own.

If you don't have the time or the inclination to build a Cardboard viewer from scratch, you can also purchase a ready-to-assemble kit from one of several manufacturers, including DODOcase (*http://www.dodocase.com/*), I Am Cardboard (*http://*

www.imcardboard.com/), Knox Labs (*http://www.knoxlabs.com/*), and Unofficial Cardboard (*https://www.unofficialcardboard.com/*). In addition to selling kits, each of these manufacturers also provides a mobile app, available to download from the Google Play Store and/or the iTunes Store, that provides a handy list of Cardboard-aware VR applications.

Figure 2-7. The original Google Cardboard VR viewer, shown at Google I/O in 2014

According to Google, over one million Cardboard viewers had shipped as of the first quarter of 2015. This number dwarfs the installed bases of the Oculus Rift and Gear VR, and on that basis alone, Cardboard is a force to be reckoned with. There are already hundreds of applications available for Cardboard, including games, 360-degree video and photo viewers, and educational simulations. Cardboard has powered VR experiences with big-name entertainers like Sir Paul McCartney and Jack White, and brands such as Volvo. So while insiders will tell you that the Cardboard VR experience isn't as deep or immersive as that of the Oculus Rift, for many people, it's going to be their first VR experience.

But Does It Have to Be Made of Cardboard?

No! Cardboard simply refers to the technique of dropping a smartphone into a box with lenses and implementing the appropriate rendering and head tracking in software. There are durable drop-in VR viewers made of other materials, including plastic and foam rubber. Chapter 6 describes several of these in detail.

Stereo Rendering and Head Tracking with Cardboard VR

The Cardboard VR approach to stereo rendering is simpler than the Rift's—it is an undistorted, 90–degree horizontal field of view. This allows applications to do simple side-by-side rendering in two viewports, one for each eye. An example of a 3D scene rendered side-by-side for Cardboard, from the game *Dive City Rollercoaster (http://bit.ly/dive-city)*, is shown in Figure 2-8.

Figure 2-8. Dive City Rollercoaster for Google Cardboard, developed by Dive Games

Head tracking for Cardboard is also straightforward. It simply uses the existing operating system orientation events generated by the phone's compass and accelerometer.

Cardboard VR Input

For Cardboard VR, input is still a work in progress. Because the phone is encased in the box, you can't touch the screen to tap or swipe. To get around this, the original Google unit featured a magnet mounted on the outside of the box that will trigger compass events that can be detected by an application. However, that combination works only with certain phone models.

Other makers of Cardboard units are developing innovations that will enable more universal input and work with most phones. For example, DODOcase, a San Francisco–based company that manufacturers tablet and phone cases, is now making a Cardboard unit that uses a wooden lever to trigger a piece of plastic that touches the surface of the phone, emulating the touch of a finger. With this mechanism, developers can use standard touch events in their VR applications. Several Cardboard makers are also experimenting with creating peripherals, such as Bluetooth-connected devices that provide simple click or swipe input.

Developing for Google Cardboard

Google provides SDKs for Cardboard developers in two forms: an Android native SDK, and an add-in for the popular Unity3D game development system. Those can be downloaded from the Android developer site (*http://bit.ly/cardboard-dev*).

We we will cover the details of building a Cardboard app using the Android SDK in Chapter 6. Note that you don't need to be an Android developer to write for Cardboard. Because most Android operating systems now support WebGL, you can actually write mobile web VR applications too! This is an exciting new area for VR development that we will cover in Chapter 5.

VR Input Devices

As we saw in Chapter 1, user input poses a new set of challenges in VR system design. With a head-mounted display completely enclosing your eyes, you can't see the physical environment around you—including your mouse or keyboard. Anyone who has tried a demo of the Oculus Rift knows all too well the feeling of your friend guiding your hands to the WASD or arrow keys so that you can use them to navigate your body through a virtual scene.

Most of the time, blind operation of the computer keyboard and mouse does not offer a good experience from a human factors point of view. With visual stimulation from the outside world cut off, we need to employ different types of input devices beyond the keyboard and mouse. A lot of experimentation is happening in this area, with the following types of input devices being used to provide a greater feeling of immersion:

- Game controllers, such as the controllers for the Microsoft Xbox One and Sony PS4 consoles. These can also be connected to desktop computers to interact with PC-based or mobile virtual reality scenes.

- Hand-tracking motion input sensors. Over the last few years, low-cost motion input devices have become available, including the Leap Motion controller (shown in Figure 2-9, mounted on the front of a DK2). The Leap Motion uses a combination of cameras and infrared LEDs to track hand motions and recognize gestures, similar to the Xbox Kinect.

- Wireless hand and body trackers, such as the full body motion STEM system by Sixense and the Hydra by Razer. These devices combine wand-like hand motion sensing with control buttons similar to those found in game controllers. Oculus is about to introduce its own such device into the market, called the Oculus Touch: a pair of lightweight wireless controllers that you hold in your hands. The Rift's positional tracking camera can locate the controllers' positions in space, so that you can see a representation of your hands in the VR world (if the app developer builds in that feature). The Oculus Touch controllers are depicted in Figure 2-10.

At this point in time, there is no one way to interact in VR using these new input devices. Much depends on the type of application being created, and the system to which the devices are connected. While it is too early to say what the "mouse of virtual reality" is going to be, it will likely emerge from products in the set described here, or devices like them. In the meantime, all this research is a big part of the fun. Expect to see a lot of innovation in this area over the next few years.

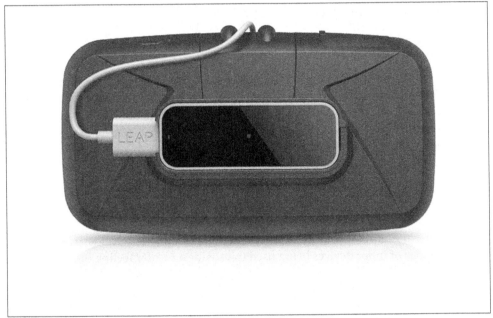

Figure 2-9. Leap Motion controller, front-mounted on the Oculus Rift DK2

Chapter Summary

Consumer VR hardware is a young and evolving field. The Oculus Rift leads this evolution with breakthrough display and head-tracking technology. Developer models are evolving rapidly, on the way toward a broad consumer releases in 2016. Each version of the Rift gets better, more ergonomic, and more consumer-friendly.

While the Oculus Rift is the standard-bearer for virtual reality, it's not the only game in town. Other manufacturers are making high-end VR headsets for desktop computers and game consoles, including the HTC Vive, Sony Morpheus for PlayStation 4, and HMDs based on OSVR, an open specification that allows manufacturers to build their own VR device.

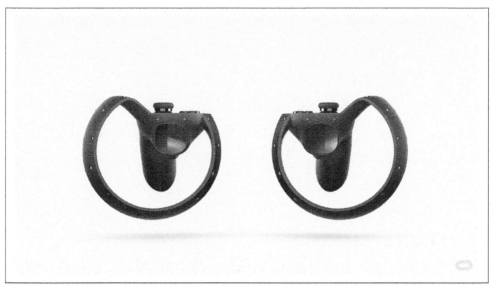

Figure 2-10. Oculus Touch controllers

For mobile virtual reality, Samsung's Gear VR, based on Oculus technology, is an outstanding product. Its high-resolution display, lightweight headset with intuitive controls, and Oculus Store user interface arguably provide the highest-quality VR experience to date. However, at a total cost of ownership that may approach US $1,000, it is currently out of reach for most consumers.

On the other end of the spectrum, Cardboard VR turns your existing smartphone into a VR device using just a few dollars' worth of parts: a cardboard box and two plastic lenses. While it may not rival the high-end experience of a Gear VR or the ultimate Oculus Rift retail release, Cardboard represents a low-cost alternative that could provide a first taste of VR for many.

Virtual reality is also pushing the envelope on user input. Because VR displays cut the user off completely from the outside world, we need to devise input systems that go beyond today's keyboard, mouse, and touch screens. Game controllers, familiar to many computer users, represent one approach; another is to look at the new generation of motion-controlled input devices from Leap Motion, Sixense, and others.

Well, that's it for our nickel tour of VR hardware. It's time to go build something.

CHAPTER 3

Going Native: Developing for Oculus Rift on the Desktop

The next several chapters cover the essentials of virtual reality development. We'll start by creating a native application for desktop computers using the Oculus Rift. While the information in this chapter is specific to the Rift and the Oculus SDK, the same techniques will apply when developing for the HTC Vive and other headsets.

In programming our first VR application, we will explore these core concepts:

Constructing a 3D scene
> We'll see how to create the visual, interactive, and scripted elements that represent the virtual reality environment.

Rendering the 3D scene in stereo
> We'll look at how to render the scene from each of two cameras representing the user's eyes. Via the lenses in the Oculus Rift headset, the two rendered images are combined into a single, coherent visual field to create a stereoscopic view of the environment.

Head tracking to provide presence
> We'll see how to use the position and orientation of the Oculus Rift headset to change the virtual camera's position and orientation within the environment.

To illustrate these ideas, we need to write 3D code. Programming to a 3D rendering API like OpenGL or DirectX is a lot of work, and is beyond the scope of this book. Instead, we are going to use the popular Unity3D (*https://unity3d.com*) game engine. Unity provides enough power to build games and VR quickly without too steep of a learning curve.

But before we delve into Unity, let's make sure we understand the basics of 3D graphics. If you are already familiar with 3D programming concepts, feel free to skip the next section.

3D Graphics Basics

Given that you picked up this book, chances are you have at least an informal idea about what we are talking about when we use the term *3D graphics*. But to make sure we are clear, we are going to get formal and examine a definition. Here is the one from Wikipedia (*http://bit.ly/3d-graphics*):

> 3D computer graphics (in contrast to 2D computer graphics) are graphics that use a three-dimensional representation of geometric data (often Cartesian) that is stored in the computer for the purposes of performing calculations and rendering 2D images. Such images may be stored for viewing later or displayed in real-time.

Let's break this down into its components: 1) the data is represented in a 3D coordinate system; 2) it is ultimately drawn ("rendered") as a 2D image on, for example, a computer monitor (or in the case of VR, it is rendered as two separate 2D images, one per eye); and 3) when the 3D data changes as it is being animated or manipulated by the user, the rendered image is updated without a perceivable delay (i.e., in real time). This last part is key for creating interactive applications. In fact, it is so important that it has spawned a multibillion-dollar industry dedicated to specialized graphics hardware supporting real-time 3D rendering, with several companies you have probably heard of (such as NVIDIA, ATI, and Qualcomm) leading the charge.

3D programming requires new skills and knowledge beyond that of the typical app developer. However, armed with a little starter knowledge and the right tools, we can get going fairly quickly.

3D Coordinate Systems

If you are familiar with 2D Cartesian coordinate systems such as the window coordinates used in a Windows desktop application or iOS mobile app, then you know about x and y values. These 2D coordinates define where child windows and UI controls are located within a window, or the where virtual "pen" or "brush" draws pixels in the window when using a graphics drawing API. Similarly, 3D drawing takes place (not surprisingly) in a 3D coordinate system, where the additional coordinate, z, describes depth—i.e., how far into or out of the screen an object is drawn. If you are already comfortable with the concept of the 2D coordinate system, the transition to a 3D coordinate system should be straightforward.

The coordinate systems we will work with in this book tend to be arranged as depicted in Figure 3-1, with x running horizontally left to right, y running vertically from bottom to top, and z going in and out of the screen. The orientation of these axes is completely arbitrary, done by convention; in some systems, for example, the z-axis is the vertical axis, while y runs in and out of the screen.

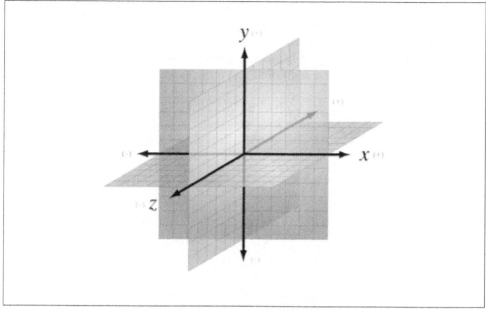

Figure 3-1. 3D coordinate system

Unity3D, the tool we will use for the examples in this chapter, follows the coordinate system depicted in Figure 3-1: z is the in/out axis, with positive z going deeper into the screen. This is known as a *lefthanded coordinate system*, versus the *righthanded coordinate system* often used in OpenGL applications, where positive z comes out of the screen.

Left Hand/Right Hand?

Remember that the orientations of the axes in 3D coordinate systems are arbitrary conventions. We will see examples of right-handed coordinates when we cover WebVR in a later chapter. Don't worry over it; it is fairly easy to make the mental transition from one system to another once you're comfortable with the general idea.

Meshes, Polygons, and Vertices

While there are several ways to draw 3D graphics, by far the most common is to use a *mesh*. A mesh is an object composed of one or more polygonal shapes, constructed out of vertices (x, y, and z triples) defining coordinate positions in 3D space. The polygons most typically used in meshes are triangles (groups of three vertices) and quads (groups of four vertices). 3D meshes are often referred to as *models*.

Figure 3-2 illustrates a 3D mesh. The dark lines outline the quads that comprise the mesh, defining the shape of the face. (You would not see these lines in the final rendered image; they are included only for reference.) The *x*, *y*, and *z* components of the mesh's vertices define the shape *only*; surface properties of the mesh, such as the color and shading, are defined using additional attributes, as we will see in the next section.

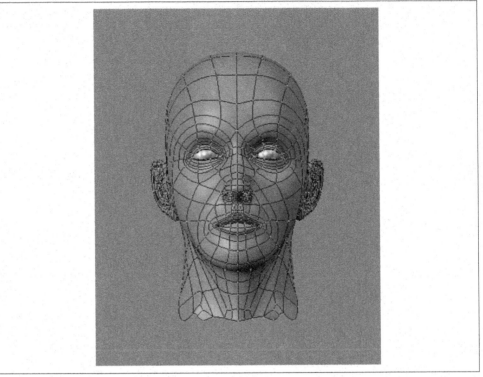

Figure 3-2. A 3D polygonal mesh

Materials, Textures, and Lights

The surface of a mesh is defined using additional attributes beyond the *x*, *y*, and *z* vertex positions. Surface attributes can be as simple as a single solid color, or they can be complex, comprising several pieces of information that define, for example, how light reflects off the object or how shiny the object looks. Surface information can also be represented using one or more bitmaps, known as *texture maps* (or simply "textures"). Textures can define the literal surface look (such as an image printed on a t-shirt), or they can be combined with other textures to achieve sophisticated effects such as bumpiness or iridescence. In most graphics systems, the surface properties of a mesh are referred to collectively as *materials*. Materials typically rely on the presence of one or more lights, which (as you may have guessed) define how a scene is illuminated.

The head depicted in Figure 3-2 has a material with a purple color and shading defined by a light source emanating from the left of the model. Note the shadows on the right side of the face.

Transforms and Matrices

3D meshes are defined by the positions of their vertices. It would get really tedious to change a mesh's vertex positions every time you wanted to move it to a different part of the view, though, especially if the mesh were continually animating. For this reason, most 3D systems support *transforms*, which are operations that move the mesh by a relative amount without having to loop through every vertex, explicitly changing its position. Transforms allow a rendered mesh to be scaled, rotated, and translated (moved), without actually changing any values in its vertices.

Figure 3-3 depicts 3D transforms in action. In this scene we see three cubes. Each of these objects is a cube mesh that contains the same values for its vertices. To move, rotate, or scale the mesh, we do not modify the vertices; rather, we apply transforms. The red cube on the left has been translated 4 units to the left (–4 on the *x*-axis), and rotated about its *x*- and *y*-axes. (Note that rotation values are specified in *radians*— units that represent the length of a circular arc on a unit circle, with 360 degrees being equal to 2 * pi.) The blue cube on the right has been translated 4 units to the right, and scaled to be 1.5 times larger in all three dimensions. The green cube in the center has not been transformed.

A 3D transform is typically represented by a *transformation matrix*, a mathematical entity containing an array of values used to compute the transformed positions of vertices. Most 3D transforms use a 4*4 matrix: that is, an array of 16 numbers organized into 4 rows and 4 columns. Figure 3-4 shows the layout of a 4*4 matrix. The translation is stored in elements m_{12}, m_{13}, and m_{14}, corresponding to the *x*, *y*, and *z* translation values. *x*, *y*, and *z* scale values are stored in elements m_0, m_5, and m_{10} (known as the diagonal of the matrix). Rotation values are stored in elements m_1 and m_2 (*x*-axis), m_4 and m_6 (*y*-axis), and m_8 and m_9 (*z*-axis). Multiplying a 3D vector by this matrix results in the transformed value.

If you are a linear algebra geek like me, you probably feel comfortable with this idea. If not, please don't break into a cold sweat. Unity3D and the other tools we will use in this book allow us to treat matrices like black boxes: we just say "translate," "rotate," or "scale," and the right thing happens. But for inquiring minds, it's good to know what is happening under the covers.

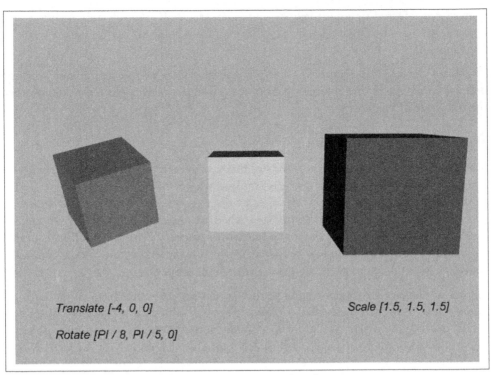

Figure 3-3. 3D transforms: translation, rotation, and scale

Cameras, Perspective, Viewports, and Projections

Every rendered scene requires a point of view from which the user will be viewing it. 3D systems typically use a camera, an object that defines where (relative to the scene) the user is positioned and oriented, as well as other real-world camera properties such as the size of the field of view, which defines perspective (i.e., objects farther away appearing smaller). The camera's properties combine to deliver the final rendered image of a 3D scene into a 2D viewport defined by the window or canvas.

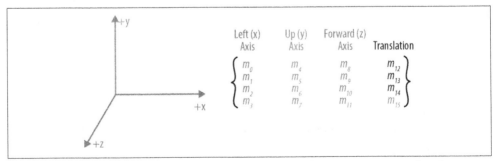

Figure 3-4. A 4*4 transformation matrix defining translation, rotation, and scale

Cameras are almost always represented using a couple of matrices. The first matrix defines the position and orientation of the camera, much like the matrix used for transforms (see the previous section). The second matrix is a specialized one that represents the translation from the 3D coordinates of the camera into the 2D drawing space of the viewport. It is called the *projection matrix*. I know: more math. But the details of camera matrices are nicely hidden in Unity3D, so you usually can just point, shoot, and render.

Figure 3-5 depicts the core concepts of the camera, viewport, and projection. At the lower left we see an icon of an eye; this represents the location of the camera. The red vector pointing to the right (in this diagram labeled as the *m*-axis) represents the direction in which the camera is pointing. The blue cubes are the objects in the 3D scene. The green and red rectangles are, respectively, the near and far clipping planes. These two planes define the boundaries of a subset of the 3D space known as the *view volume* or *view frustum*. Only objects within the view volume are actually rendered to the screen. The near clipping plane is equivalent to the viewport, where we will see the final rendered image.

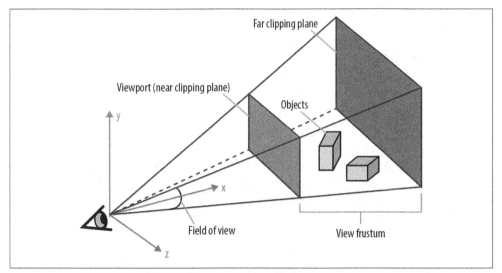

Figure 3-5. Camera, viewport, and perspective projection

Cameras are extremely powerful, as they ultimately define the viewer's relationship to a 3D scene and provide a sense of realism. They also provide another weapon in the animator's arsenal: by dynamically moving the camera around you can create cinematic effects and control the narrative experience. Of course, with VR, camera control has to be a balance between moving the user around within the scene and allowing the user the freedom of movement necessary to convey a sense of presence. We will explore this idea more in later chapters.

Stereoscopic Rendering

Rendering 3D for virtual reality adds a wrinkle to how we deal with cameras, viewports, and projection matrices. In essence we have to do the whole thing twice, once per eye. Thankfully, this is easier than it sounds. There are a few approaches to doing it, but the simplest is as follows:

1. *Define one main camera for the simulation.* The application maintains a single main camera, as if it were being rendered in mono. All animations and behaviors that affect the camera, such as terrain following, collisions, or VR head tracking, are performed on this one main camera. This provides a simple and consistent way to deal with the camera as an object, separate from the concerns of rendering. It also allows the developer to easily create both stereo and mono versions of the same application, when that is appropriate.
2. *Render from two cameras.* The application maintains two additional cameras, which are used only to render the scene. These cameras always follow the position and orientation of the main camera, but are slightly offset to the left and right of it, to mimic the user's interpupillary distance.
3. *Render to two viewports.* The application creates separate viewports for the left and right rendering cameras. Each viewport is half the width of the full screen, and the full height. The graphics for each camera are rendered to the respective viewport using a projection matrix set up specifically for each eye, using the optical distortion parameters of the device (provided by the Oculus SDK).

And there you have it: the basics of 3D graphics for VR, in a few pages. There is a lot of stuff to get right, and even the simplest details can take time to master. Also, as you scale up your development from simple to more complex applications, you will want to do more without having to get mired in low-level coding. For these reasons, it is best to use a game engine. You can write an engine of your own, if you're so inclined; but if you're like me, you would rather spend your time working on the application itself and just use an existing engine. Thankfully, there are several good ones, including the subject of the next section, Unity3D.

Unity3D: The Game Engine for the Common Man

Not all virtual reality applications are games. However, professional game engines have become a tool of choice for developing virtual reality, because of the close fit between the capabilities of the engines and the requirements for creating good VR. Game engines provide a host of features, including high-quality rendering, physics simulations, real-time lighting, scripting, and powerful WYSIWYG editors.

While there are several great game engines on the market, Unity3D from Unity Technologies seems to be the go-to solution for VR. Unity has emerged as the preferred tool for indie and hobbyist game development, due to its combination of power and accessibility at a great price. Highlights of Unity3D include:

Power

The Unity player runtime provides many important graphics features, such as a rich material system with physically based rendering, real-time lighting, physics, and scripted behaviors.

Extensibility

Unity is based on an entities-and-components model that makes the system flexible, extensible, and configurable via user scripts; even the editor's features can be overriden, allowing for the creation of custom editing tools.

WYSIWYG editor

The Unity editor can be daunting at first, but once you are familiar with it, you will find it easy to use. The editor supports many productivity features and workflows, and can import models and scenes from professional tools like Autodesk Maya and 3ds Max.

Portablilty

The player runtime supports running on native desktop platforms (OS X, Windows, Linux), popular game consoles such as Xbox and PlayStation, mobile operating systems including iOS and Android, and the Web via both a player plugin and experimental support for WebGL. This means that developers can invest the time to learn and master Unity and be assured that they can port their work to other environments.

Affordability

The free version of Unity is fully featured. For commercial use, the company offers reasonable licensing terms that include an affordable monthly fee and a modest royalty—but only if you are charging for your application.

Rich ecosystem

Unity has an online Asset Store (*http://bit.ly/unity-asset*) featuring countless 3D models, animations, code packages, and utilities. The Asset Store is in a large way responsible for Unity having one of the most vibrant developer communities on the planet.

Ready for VR

The Unity engine contains native support for VR rendering and head tracking. The Oculus Utilities for Unity package, available for download from the Oculus developer site (*https://developer.oculus.com/*), provides support for key virtual reality programming constructs and sample scenes and code to get you started.

To work with the samples in this chapter, you will need to download and install Unity on your computer. Go to the download page (*http://unity3d.com/get-unity*) and follow the instructions.

Once installed, launch Unity, create a new, empty 3D project, and explore the product. Figure 3-6 shows an OS X screenshot of the Unity interface. There is a main Scene view, which can be configured into a four-view layout (left, top, right, and perspective) or other types of layouts. The Hierarchy pane lets you browse through the objects in the current scene. The Project pane shows you a view of all the assets currently in your project—these may or may not be loaded into the current scene. The Inspector pane provides detailed property information and the ability to edit properties for the currently selected object.

The examples in this book were developed using Unity version 5. As of this writing, the current version (found in the Unity About dialog) is 5.1.2f1.

Is Unity the Only Way to Make VR?

You may be wondering if Unity is the only game in town when it comes to creating VR applications. The short answer is, "no." You can always use the capabilities of the Oculus SDK to write your own native application in C++, using OpenGL or DirectX. Or you can use any of a number of other great commercial engines, such as the Unreal Engine (*http://bit.ly/unreal-engine-4*) or Crytek's CRYENGINE (*http://cryengine.com/*). For more information on these products, see Appendix A.

Setting Up the Oculus SDK

Before you can use a tool like Unity3D to develop for the Oculus Rift, you also need to install the Oculus SDK, which is available on the Oculus developer website. (*https://developer.oculus.com/*)

If you don't have an account, sign up; it's free. Once you are logged in to the site, do the following:

1. Select Downloads from the top navigation bar.
2. Under the SDK Runtime section, click the Details button to the right of *Oculus Runtime for Windows V0.6.0.1-beta*. Agree to the terms of the end-user license agreement (EULA) and click Download.
3. Run the installer for the Oculus runtime on your PC.
4. Under the SDK Runtime section, click the Details button to the right of *Oculus SDK for Windows V0.6.0.1-beta*. Agree to the terms of EULA and click Download.
5. Unzip the SDK to your hard drive, in a location of your choice.

6. While you're here, grab the Unity package for Oculus. Under the Engine Integration section, download *Oculus Utilities for Unity 5 V0.1.0-beta* by clicking the Details button, agreeing to the terms of EULA, and clicking Download.
7. Unzip the Oculus Utilities package to your hard drive, in a location of your choice.

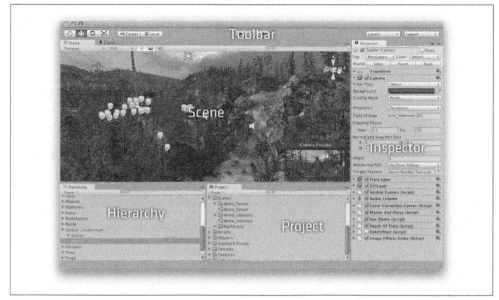

Figure 3-6. Unity3D editor interface (source: official product documentation (http://bit.ly/unity3d-docs))

Let's do one more setup step to make sure that the Oculus Rift display driver for Windows is in the correct mode. Launch the Oculus configuration utility from Windows Explorer. (in my setup, this is located at *Program Files (x86)\Oculus\Tools\Oculus-ConfigUtil.exe*. There are a few options, as depicted in Figure 3-7. Make sure that "Direct HMD Access from Apps" is selected.

A good way to test that your setup worked is to run the demo program included with the SDK. Find the location on your computer where you installed the Oculus SDK, and open *OculusWorldDemo.exe*. Put on your Rift, and you should see the Tuscan village demo depicted in Chapter 1. Welcome to Italy! Enjoy your stay.

With the Oculus runtime and SDK installations complete, we can move on to setting up Unity3D for use with the SDK.

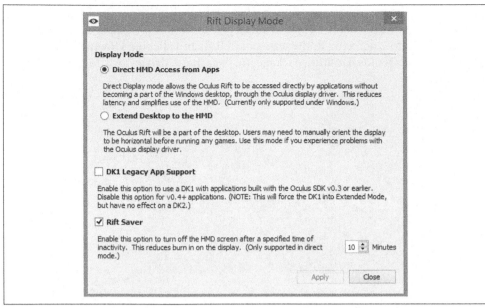

Figure 3-7. Selecting the Rift display mode from the Oculus configuration utility

The Oculus SDK on Non-Windows Platforms

The Oculus SDK is currently only supported on Windows; OS X and Linux support was mothballed in early 2015. As a result, Unity's support for Oculus on non-Windows platforms is also on hold. This situation will potentially change, but as of this writing, it is best to use Unity3D to develop for Oculus on Windows. If you have a Mac or Linux machine you can follow along, but unless you installed the Oculus SDK prior to the spring of 2015 (or can find an older version for download on the developer site), you won't be able to run the examples using those platforms.

Setting Up Your Unity Environment for Oculus Development

Now that you have downloaded the Oculus runtime, the SDK, and the Oculus Utilities for Unity package, you are ready to start developing for Unity. You do that by importing the Utilities package into a Unity project. Let's start by creating an empty Unity project. Launch Unity3D, or if it is already running, select File → New Project.

Name your new project *UnityOculusTest*. Now that the project has been created, we will import the SDK into it and build a simple application.

Figure 3-8 shows a screenshot of the package importing process. To import the Oculus Utilities package into the new project, follow these steps:

1. Find the Assets pane of the Project tab in the Unity IDE. Choose Assets → Import Package → Custom Package.
2. You should see a file dialog box. Use it to navigate to the location of the downloaded Oculus Utilities package.
3. Select the file *OculusUtilities.unitypackage*.
4. Once you have clicked Open, Unity will scan the file and present you with a list of package contents to import. For now, let's just bring them all into the project: make sure that all of the objects in the list are checked, and click the Import button. You will now see assets present in the Assets pane, where there were none before. In particular, you should see folders named *OVR* and *Plugins*.

Figure 3-8. Importing the Oculus Utilities package into a Unity project

You now have a Unity project ready to go for building an Oculus application. Let's get into it.

Building Your First VR Example

Once you have imported the Oculus Utilities package into your project, you are ready to build your first desktop VR sample. The package comes with example content, and when you're done with importing, that content will now be in your project. In just a few steps you can have it running on your computer. The demo we are going to build is pictured in Figure 3-9, a screenshot from my PC laptop. It is a simple scene with hundreds of cubes floating in space. When you attach the Oculus Rift to your computer, you will be immersed in a view of this scene. Turn your head left, right, up, and down; there are cubes everywhere you look!

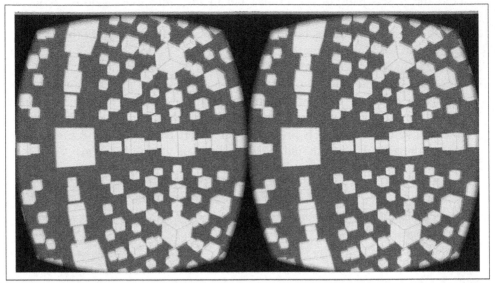

Figure 3-9. Unity Cubes example running in Oculus Rift

Let's build and run this example.

To get the assets for Cubes World application built into your new project, select the folder *Assets/OVR/Scenes* in the Project pane of the Unity interface. In the detail pane you will see an icon for a Unity scene named *Cubes*; double-click that icon. You should now see the scene in the main editor view. Figure 3-10 shows the Unity editor with a four-view layout of the *Cubes* scene (left, right, top, and perspective).

To get a quick preview on your main monitor, make sure you have "Maximize on Play" selected in the Game window (bottom left of the four panes in the four-view layout) then click the Play button at the top of the Unity window. You should see something like the screenshot in Figure 3-11.

Now let's get the application running on the Rift.

Building and Running the Application

Unity supports creating games for a variety of target environments, including native desktop platforms, the Web (using their proprietary player plugin), WebGL (experimental), mobile platforms like iOS and Android, and game consoles such as Xbox and PlayStation.

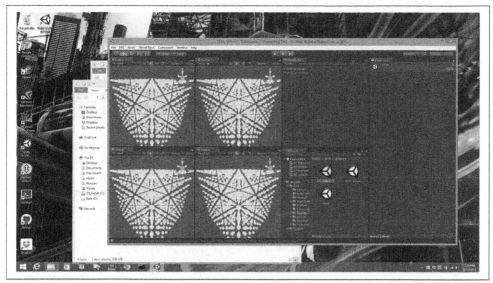

Figure 3-10. Cubes scene viewed in the Unity3D editor

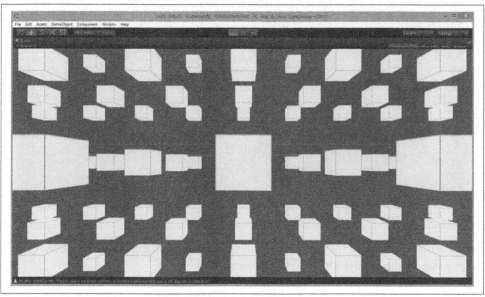

Figure 3-11. Unity player preview of Cubes World

To build and run the Cubes World application for the desktop, first select File → Build Settings. You will see a dialog like the one depicted in Figure 3-12.

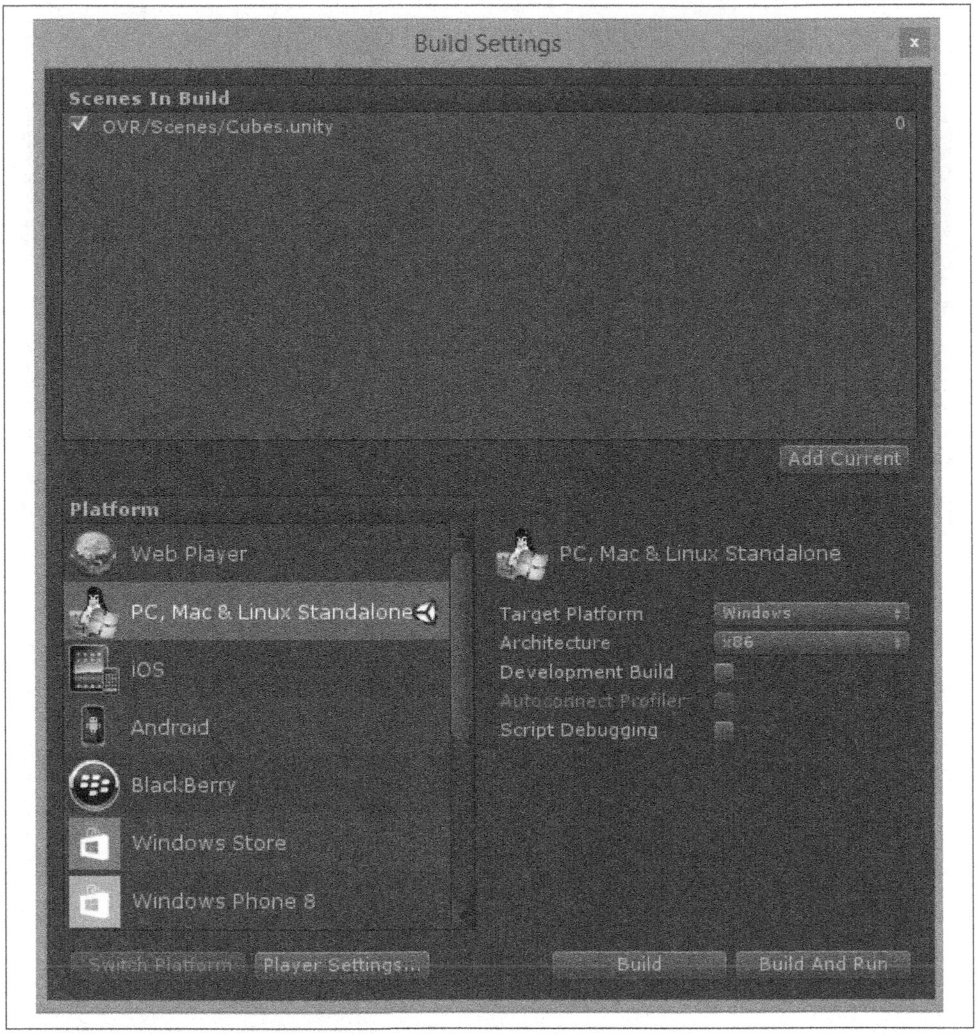

Figure 3-12. Unity3D build settings

Now perform the following steps—and make sure you remember these steps for setting up subsequent Unity Oculus Rift projects:

1. Select "PC, Mac & Linux Standalone" in the list of platforms, and then click the Switch Platform button.
2. Make sure Target Platform is set to Windows in the combo box on the right.
3. Add the demo scene to your build. The Scenes In Build list at the top will be empty to start; you need to add the current scene. You should already be viewing it in the editor view, so if you click the Add Current button, it should be added to the list. You will then see a checked item named *OVR/Scenes/Cubes.unity*.

4. Click the Player Settings button. This will bring up a variety of settings in the Inspector pane. Select the Other Settings subpane at the bottom, and check the box labeled Virtual Reality Supported. This turns on Unity's built-in VR support, which, combined with the capabilities of the Oculus Utilities package, gives you everything you need to run VR applications in Unity.

5. Back in the Build Settings dialog, click the Build And Run button. You will be prompted for a filename under which to save the executable. (I named mine *OculusUnityTest.exe*, but this is up to you.)

Assuming you didn't get any build errors, the application should launch. If you haven't yet connected the Rift, you will see the Cubes World app rendering fullscreen in monoscopic mode, and it won't be responsive to your mouse or any other input. If this is the case, press Alt-F4 to exit the app, then connect the Rift and try again.

If your Rift is already connected, you should see the application launch in fullscreen mode, with the standard Oculus VR health and safety startup screen as depicted in Figure 3-13. Press a key, pop the Rift on your head, and go.

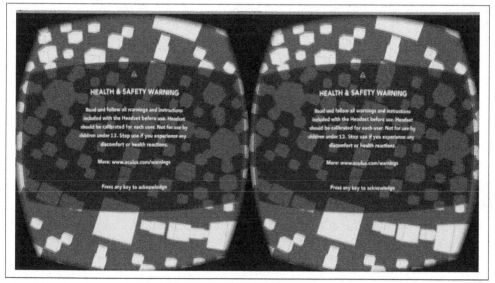

Figure 3-13. Cubes World startup screen, successfully launched on the PC

You can also use the Play button at the top of the Unity window to preview the application, even in VR mode. In preview mode, you will see a scene like the screenshot in Figure 3-11 on your main monitor; on the Rift, you will see the correct scene rendered and head-tracked in VR.

Congratulations. You've just built your first VR application! Now let's have a look at how it works.

Walking Through the Code

The easiest way to use Unity for VR development is to import the Oculus Utilities package, as we did in the previous section. The package comes with several helper objects and samples, most notably a *camera rig* prefab. (*Prefab* is a Unity term for a set of prebuilt objects that can be used together as a unit.) The camera rig prefab is responsible for interfacing between Unity's built-in Oculus stereo rendering and head tracking—the essential elements of the VR experience—and the application. Let's take a look at how it is constructed.

In the Hierarchy pane, locate the *OVRCameraRig* object, and expand it by clicking the down arrow icon to the left of the name. The camera rig contains a child object, *TrackingSpace*. Expand that, and you'll see four children: *LeftEyeAnchor*, *Center-EyeAnchor*, *RightEyeAnchor*, and *TrackerAnchor*. The center anchor is the key: it contains the camera setup for the application, which is used by the built-in Unity VR support to render the view from the left and right eyes, respectively. The Unity engine copies the camera parameters from the center anchor's camera to the left and right cameras it uses internally to render the scene. You can see in the Inspector pane by selecting *CenterEyeAnchor* that it contains a camera component with values for projection, field of view, background (used to paint the scene's background color for each render cycle), and so on.

The *TrackerAnchor* is there so that the application can always know the current position and orientation of the camera. This is useful in a variety of scenarios. Perhaps we want to have objects that are always placed relative to the camera at a certain distance; in this way we can properly place them whenever the camera moves. Or maybe we are creating a networked multiplayer game. For that, it is crucial to know where each player is and in which direction he is looking. The left and right anchors are there for completeness, so that we always have the individual position and orientation of the left and right cameras if we need that information (more on this shortly).

To get a feel for how the anchor objects are implemented, let's look at some Unity script code. In the Hierarchy pane, select the object *OVRCameraRig* again. You'll see that it contains a few script components. We want to look at the properties for the component labeled *OVR Camera Rig (Script)*. Its Script property has the value *OVR-CameraRig*. Double-click on that value and MonoDevelop, Unity's code editor for C# programmers, will open the source file *OVRCameraRig.cs* from the project sources.

About the C# Language

The examples in this section assume basic familiarity with C#. If you're not acquainted with this language, see "Programming Languages" on page 139.

In the MonoDevelop source code window, scroll through or search until you find the definition of the method Update(), shown here:

```
private void Update()
{
    EnsureGameObjectIntegrity();

    if (!Application.isPlaying)
        return;

    UpdateAnchors();

#if UNITY_ANDROID && !UNITY_EDITOR

    // ... code omitted ...
#endif
}
```

The camera rig's Update() method first calls a helper, EnsureGameObjectInteg rity(), to make sure that the scene contains all of the required objects (that is, the objects defined in the *OVRCameraRig* prefab). This is necessary because the script component might have been included in a project without the rest of the prefab. If this is the case, the script knows how to reconstruct the other objects in the prefab so that all the code still works. In our example we actually included the whole prefab, so the method call isn't really necessary, but you should be aware that the script has been designed with that robustness in mind.

After a check to see whether the application is actually running—it may not be, either because it hasn't been set into run mode yet or because the object is being viewed in the Unity editor and not in play mode—we do some real work. We need to position and orient the anchor objects based on where the Oculus Rift HMD is looking. This is done in the method UpdateAnchors():

```
private void UpdateAnchors()
{
    bool monoscopic = OVRManager.instance.monoscopic;

    OVRPose tracker = OVRManager.tracker.GetPose(0d);

    trackerAnchor.localRotation = tracker.orientation;
    centerEyeAnchor.localRotation =
    VR.InputTracking.GetLocalRotation(VR.VRNode.CenterEye);
    leftEyeAnchor.localRotation = monoscopic ?
            centerEyeAnchor.localRotation :
            VR.InputTracking.GetLocalRotation(VR.VRNode.LeftEye);
    rightEyeAnchor.localRotation = monoscopic ?
            centerEyeAnchor.localRotation :
            VR.InputTracking.GetLocalRotation(VR.VRNode.RightEye);

    trackerAnchor.localPosition = tracker.position;
```

```
centerEyeAnchor.localPosition =
VR.InputTracking.GetLocalPosition(VR.VRNode.CenterEye);
leftEyeAnchor.localPosition = monoscopic ?
        centerEyeAnchor.localPosition :
        VR.InputTracking.GetLocalPosition(VR.VRNode.LeftEye);
rightEyeAnchor.localPosition = monoscopic ?
        centerEyeAnchor.localPosition :
        VR.InputTracking.GetLocalPosition(VR.VRNode.RightEye);

if (UpdatedAnchors != null)
{
    UpdatedAnchors(this);
}
}
```

Note the test for monoscopic mode. The Oculus Utilities package has been designed to work whether or not the application is running in stereo mode. This helps with debugging, as well as demoing on flat screens. If we are running in monoscopic mode, we will simply copy the position and orientation values of the HMD from the center eye values to the left and right, rather than calculating left and right eye positions and orientations individually.

UpdateAnchors() uses the OVRManager's helper object, OVRTracker, to obtain the positional tracker's current *pose*, or position and orientation. The camera rig stores this information in the local position and orientation of its trackerAnchor child object by setting the localPosition and localRotation properties of that object. trackerAnchor is the "virtual camera" used by other parts of the application that might want to know where the camera is, as described previously.

The left and right anchors always maintain the current pose of the left and right rendering cameras, respectively, in case the application wants to access those values individually. The center anchor represents the point midway between those two anchors, with the corresponding orientation. The camera rig code uses the Unity package VR.InputTracking to obtain these values via the GetLocalRotation() and GetLocalPosition() methods, passing in an enumerated type representing left, right, or center.

The final lines of code in UpdateAnchors() will generate an event if the object has been assigned an event listener. Unity has a rich system that allows objects to listen to each other for notifications of when interesting things (*events*) happen: for example, in our case, the application might want to know when the HMD's pose values change. The OVRCameraRig class defines an event, UpdatedAnchors (note the "d" in there for past tense), that an application can listen for in script code. A Unity event listener is a function with a void return type, defined as a C# generic type. For example, here is the definition of the camera rig's UpdatedAnchors event:

```
public event System.Action<OVRCameraRig> UpdatedAnchors;
```

If the application has set the `UpdatedAnchors` property on the `OVRCameraRig` object in the scene, Unity will automatically call that function whenever the HMD moves or rotates.

One last thing about the camera rig. You may have noticed that the script makes use of another C# class, `OVRManager`. This class is the main interface to Unity's built-in Oculus support. It is responsible for doing a lot, including interfacing with native code in the Oculus SDK. If you're curious about what's in `OVRManager`, you can go back to the Unity editor and select the *OVRCameraRig* object from the Hierarchy pane; you will see that it has a second script component, *OVR Manager (Script)*. Double-click the Script property's value to open the C# source in MonoDevelop (file *OVRManager.cs*). Take a browse through the source if you like. For now, we are going to treat it as a black box.

And that's it. By changing one setting in the Unity editor interface, and adding a single prefab, you can add Oculus Rift stereo rendering and head tracking to your app. The code underneath is complex, and if you dig deep through the Unity sources you will discover a lot of arcana. But it works, and this simple example illustrates how to create desktop VR using Unity3D.

Chapter Summary

In this chapter we created our first virtual reality application for desktop PCs using the Oculus Rift. We examined the tools and techniques for developing VR, including constructing a 3D scene, rendering in stereo, and head tracking to convey presence. This chapter also included a brief primer on 3D graphics to provide an understanding of general 3D programming concepts, as well as those specific to virtual reality.

We explored using Unity3D, the powerful, affordable game engine that is becoming a de facto choice for developing VR applications. Unity saves us time and hassle over writing our own native 3D code, and provides several productivity and workflow features. Unity's built-in VR support automatically handles stereo rendering and head tracking. The Oculus developer site also offers for download a ready-to-go Utilities for Unity package that includes code for handling common VR tasks, and prebuilt VR scenes to get us going quickly.

Armed with a basic understanding of 3D, the core concepts of VR development, and the power of Unity, we were able to get started programming virtual reality. Much of the rest of the book is variations on these themes. From here, we will look at other platforms and tools, before diving headlong into building a full, real VR application.

CHAPTER 4

Going Mobile: Developing for Gear VR

In this chapter, we will learn to develop virtual reality applications for the flagship mobile device on the market today, Samsung's Gear VR. The ideas we covered in the previous chapter on desktop VR translate directly into programming for mobile, but there are also unique concerns relating to the Android platform used to develop for the Gear VR. Once again, we will use the Unity3D engine to build our examples. But before we get into the details of coding, let's explore this revolutionary new device.

In partnership with Oculus, Samsung has created a mobile VR solution that combines Oculus optics (the barrel distortion lenses) with new head-tracking technology, placed in a custom headset that houses a smartphone with a high-resolution display. Samsung released an "Innovator Edition" of the Gear VR in late 2014 for the Galaxy Note 4 phone, and another in early 2015 for the S6 line. The Gear VR unit costs US $199 and can be purchased through Samsung's online store (*http://bit.ly/samsung-wearable*). It only works with those phones, so this is not only a potentially pricey option (the phones can cost from US$600–$800 without a two-year plan), but also a restrictive one—at least for now. Still, the Gear VR is the highest-quality mobile VR on the market and provides a wonderful experience.

The Gear VR Innovator Edition for S6 phones is depicted in Figure 4-1.

The Gear VR features high-resolution graphics, with a display resolution of 2560*1440 pixels (1280*1440 per eye) in both Note 4 and S6 phones. The headset contains a custom IMU based on Oculus technology that tracks much faster and with less latency than the IMU built into the phone.

The Gear VR housing has several intuitive input controls, including an eye adjustment wheel (for matching the device's interpupillary distance to your own), and several controls that let you access the phone within: a volume control, a headphone jack, and, most importantly, a trackpad for touch input, known as the *touchpad*.

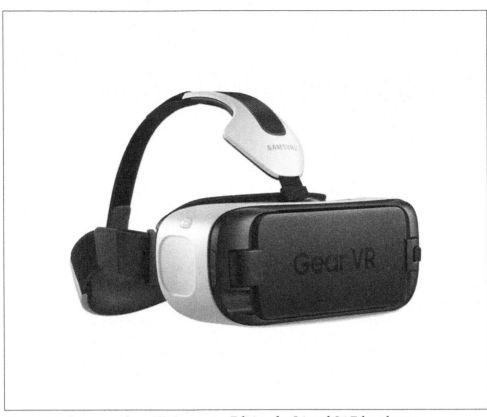

Figure 4-1. Samsung Gear VR Innovator Edition for S6 and S6 Edge phones

The Gear VR User Interface and Oculus Home

Beyond the big breakthroughs in ergonomics and resolution, the Gear VR features an innovative user interface for discovering, launching, and installing mobile VR applications called *Oculus Home*. Oculus Home is an app, but it is also a set of improvements to Samsung's mobile operating system.

Oculus Home provides a completely immersive interface for browsing VR applications, so that you don't have to remove the headset to launch a new app. While inside the store interface, you can also see system alerts for new emails, text messages, notifications, and so on. The net result is that you can have an uninterrupted VR experience, moving between applications and staying in there as long as you like, all while not being cut off from the other important goings-on of your phone.

A screenshot of Oculus Home is shown in Figure 4-2, with the Store interface selected, allowing you to browse for new apps to install.

Figure 4-2. Oculus Home for Gear VR

Using the Oculus Mobile SDK

Developing applications for the Gear VR's Android-based operating system requires the Oculus Mobile SDK, which is available on the Oculus developer website (*https://developer.oculus.com/*).

If you don't have an account, sign up; it's free. Once you are logged in to the site, do the following:

1. Select Downloads from the top navigation bar.
2. Under the SDK Runtime section, click the Details button to the right of *Oculus Mobile SDK V0.6.0.1*. Agree to the terms of the EULA and click Download.
3. Unzip the SDK to your hard drive, in a location of your choice. I put mine in the */Applications* folder on my MacBook.
4. While you're here, grab the Unity package for Oculus. Under the Engine Integration section, download *Oculus Utilities for Unity 5 V0.1.0-beta* by clicking the Details button, agreeing to the EULA, and clicking Download.
5. Unzip the Oculus Utilities package to your hard drive, in a location of your choice. Again, I unzipped mine to my */Applications* folder.

Setting Up the Android SDK

To develop applications that will work on the Gear VR, you need to use the Android SDK in conjunction with the Oculus Mobile SDK. To set up the Android SDK, go to *http://bit.ly/install-android-sdk.*

You can install the standalone SDK Tools, or you can get Android Studio. This is your choice. We will be using Android Studio for our Java work in Chapter 6, but you can always set that up later and just go with the standalone SDK Tools for now.

You will also want to learn about the Android debugging tools, because you may need to use them on the command line. There is a good write-up on these tools at *http://bit.ly/android-debugging.*

Generating an Oculus Signature File

You will need a signature file to run applications on your device. Applications that access the VR functionality of the Oculus Mobile SDK must be built with a unique signature in order to access low-level device functions through APIs provided by the SDK. This is not how you will deploy applications in practice—only properly signed Android package files (APKs) are needed as part of the Oculus Store deployment process—but it is required for deploying on your development devices during testing.

An online signature file generating tool is available at *http://bit.ly/oculus-osig.* It contains detailed instructions for how to obtain your device ID and use that to generate a signature file. Essentially, you have to run the following command in a terminal (shell) window:

```
adb
```

This command will print a unique ID for your device. Copy that ID and enter it into the field at the top of the signature tool page, and you will get a file to download. Once you have downloaded that file, squirrel it away in a safe place on your computer; you will need it for all Gear VR development, regardless of which development tool you decide to use.

Setting Up Your Device for USB Debugging

You will also need to set up USB debugging on your device in order to build and deploy applications to it. There's a trick to it, essentially an Easter egg in the Note 4 or S6 phone's settings: go to Settings → General → About Device, and tap on your build number seven times (for further details, see *http://bit.ly/enable-dev-mode*).

Once you have done all the above steps outlined here, you're ready to use the Oculus Mobile SDK to develop Gear VR applications. Please be patient; Android setup can be tricky, and the Oculus Mobile SDK adds a few extra wrinkles.

Developing for Gear VR Using Unity3D

In the last chapter we learned about creating desktop Oculus Rift applications using Unity3D, the powerful, affordable game engine from Unity Technologies. We can also use Unity3D to create applications for Gear VR, using the Oculus Mobile SDK.

Do I Have to Use Unity?

You may be wondering if Unity3D is the only way to build for Gear VR. The short answer is, "no." Gear VR development is, ultimately, Android development. Unity has several features that make Android development easier, especially for creating games and virtual reality. But if you are not a Unity developer, or if you prefer writing native Android code over using middleware, you have other options. One such option is *GearVRf (http://www.gearvrf.org/)*, a native Java framework created by Samsung and recently released as an open source library.

Setting Up Your Unity3D Environment

Now that you have downloaded the Oculus Mobile SDK, set up your Android environment, and created a signature file, you are ready to start using the Oculus Utilities for Unity package. (If you have not already done so, please download the package from the Oculus developer site, as described in the previous section.) You do this by importing the package into a Unity project. Let's start by creating an empty Unity project. Launch Unity3D, or if it is already running, select File → New Project.

Name your new project *UnityGearVRTest*. Now that the project has been created, we will import the SDK into it and build a simple application.

Figure 4-3 shows a screenshot of the package importing process. To import the Oculus Utilities package into the new project, follow these steps:

1. Find the Assets pane of the Project tab in the Unity IDE. Choose Assets → Import Package → Custom Package.
2. You should see a file dialog box. Use it to navigate to the location of the downloaded Oculus Utilities package (on my MacBook it's *Applications/OculusUtilities_0_1_0_beta/*).
3. Select the file *OculusUtilities.unitypackage*.
4. Once you have clicked Open, Unity will scan the file and present you with a list of package contents to import. For now, let's just bring them all into the project: make sure that all of the objects in the list are checked, and click the Import button. You will now see assets present in the Assets pane, where there were none before. In particular, you should see folders named *OVR* and *Plugins*.

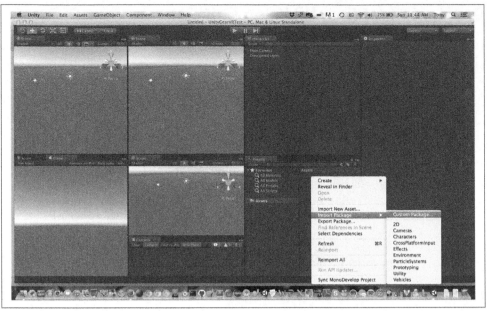

Figure 4-3. Importing the Oculus Utilities package into a Unity project

You're good to go! You can now build Gear VR applications using Unity.

A Simple Unity3D Sample

Once you have imported the Oculus Utilities package into your project, you are ready to build your first Gear VR sample. The package comes with example content, which will be included in your project. In just a few steps you can have it running on your phone. The demo we are going to build is pictured in Figure 4-4, a screenshot from my Note 4 phone before inserting it into the Gear VR headset.

To add the assets for the Cubes World application to your new project, select the folder *Assets/OVR/Scenes* in the Project pane of the Unity interface. In the detail pane you will see an icon for a Unity scene named *Cubes*; double-click that icon. You should now see the scene in the main editor view. You can hit the Play button at the top of the Unity window to get a preview on your computer.

Now, to build the app for your phone, you will need to adjust some settings. First, open the Build Settings dialog by selecting File → Build Settings from the main menu. You will see a dialog that resembles the screenshot in Figure 4-5.

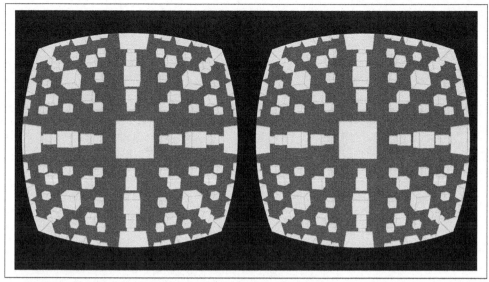

Figure 4-4. Cubes World: a simple Gear VR application built with Unity3D

Now perform the following steps (making sure to remember these steps for setting up subsequent Unity Gear VR projects):

1. Select Android in the list of platforms on the left, then click the Switch Platform button.
2. Add the demo scene to your build. The Scenes In Build list at the top will be empty to start; you need to add the current scene. You should already be viewing it in the editor view; clicking the Add Current button will add it to the list, and you will see a checked item named *OVR/Scenes/Cubes.unity*.
3. Click the Player Settings button on the bottom left. This will bring up a variety of settings in the Inspector pane. Select the Other Settings subpane at the bottom, and check the box labeled Virtual Reality Supported. This turns on Unity's built-in VR support, which, combined with the capabilities of the Oculus Utilities package, gives you everything you need run Gear VR applications in Unity.
4. In Player Settings, find the Bundle Identifier setting, and change its value to a reasonable Android package name. Make sure to change it from the default value, or Unity will complain during the build step. I used the value *vr.GearVR.UnityGearVRTest*.
5. In Player Settings, find the combo box labeled Minimum API Level and change it to "Android 4.4 'KitKat' (API level 19)" or higher.

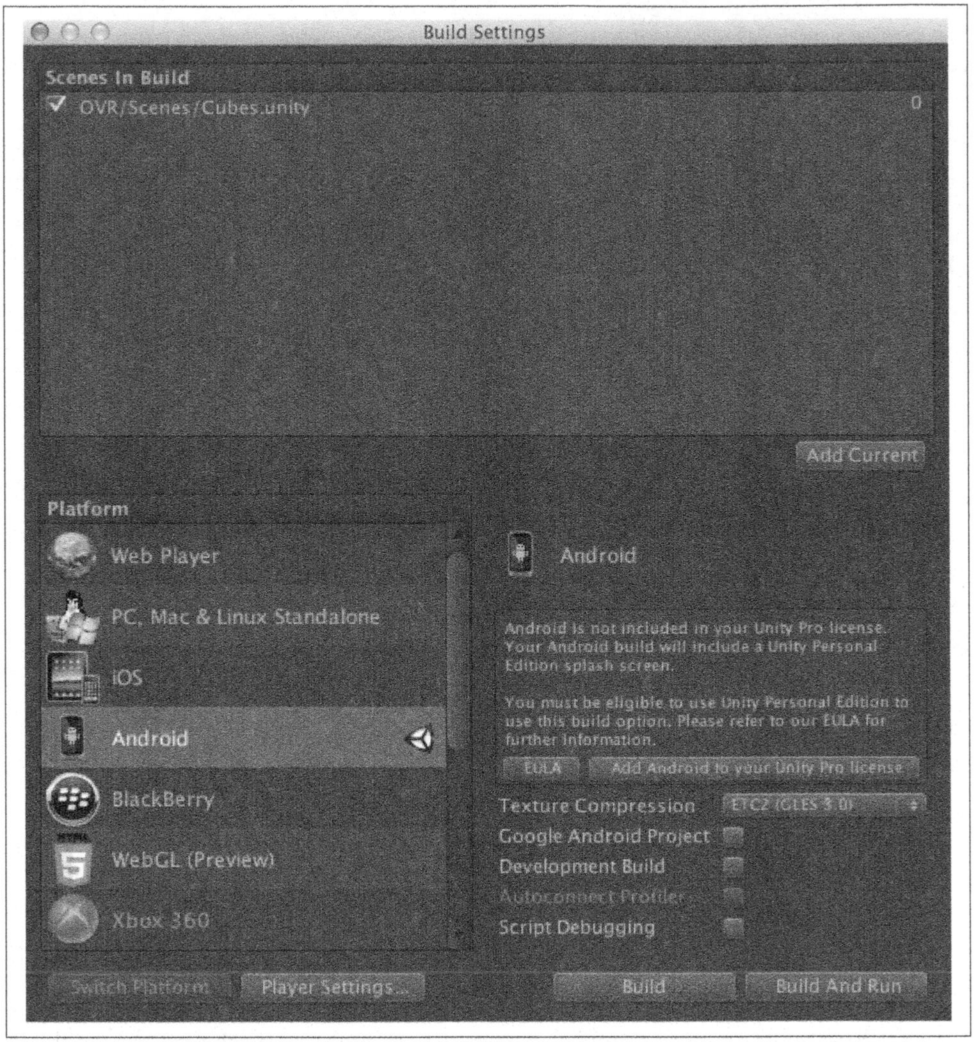

Figure 4-5. Build settings for the Cubes World Android app

There is one final thing you need to do so that you can run the project on your phone. To run Gear VR applications built with the Oculus SDK, you will need a signature file. If you haven't already, follow the instructions given earlier in the chapter and generate a signature file for your device. Once you have that, squirrel it away in a safe place; you will need it for all Gear VR development.

Each Unity3D project needs a copy of the signature file put in a known place in the build: specifically, *Assets/Plugins/Android/assets* (note the lowercase "a" in that last folder name). You can either drag and drop the file from your desktop folder into the folder in the Project pane within the Unity interface, or copy the file using your operating system interface, locate the folder where your Unity project is stored, and paste it there. (On my MacBook, that is the path *<username>/Unity Projects/Unity-GearVRTest/Assets/Plugins/Android/assets.*)

A Note About Unity and Oculus Mobile SDK Versions

Mileage may vary, and depending on which versions of the various tools you're using you may have to change more, or fewer, options than described here. I used Unity 5 (build 5.1.2f1) on my MacBook running OS X, version 0.6.0.1 of the Oculus Mobile SDK, and version 0.1.0 of the Oculus Utilities (*OculusUtilities_0_1_0_beta*).

OK! If you got through all that, you should be ready to build and run the app for your phone. Make sure to connect your computer to your device with a USB cable, and that the device is set up for USB debugging (as described earlier in the chapter). Now, hit Build And Run in the Build Settings dialog. You will be prompted for a filename under which to save the *.apk* (Android package) file. I chose the name *Unity-GearVRTest.apk*. That's the name that will show up on the phone in your list of apps. Hit Save to save the *.apk*. The app should now launch, showing the split-screen Oculus distortion view from Figure 4-4. Disconnect the cable, pop the phone into your Gear VR headset, and go. You should be inside a world of cubes, and when you move your head, you will be looking around the scene. Welcome to mobile virtual reality!

Gear VR Developer Mode

When you launched your application, you may have seen an alert pop up on your phone prompting you to insert the device into your Gear VR. By default, the Gear VR Service—that is, the software that interfaces between your Android phone and the Gear VR hardware—is set up to force you to insert the phone into the Gear VR. You can turn this off by going to your phone's settings. Launch the settings, then choose Applications/Application Manager/Gear VR Service. You will see a button labeled Manage Storage; press that and set the Developer Mode toggle to On. Now, when you launch a Gear VR application from your phone's home screen, it will run in stereo split screen mode as depicted in Figure 4-4.

Now it's time to explore the inner workings of the Oculus Utilities package for Gear VR. The Oculus team has managed to create a single code base that runs on both desktop platforms and the Gear VR, so this is exactly the same code as in the desktop example from Chapter 3, with just a few small differences for running on the Gear VR.

First, let's see how the Unity scene is set up. The Oculus Utilities package comes with a camera rig prefab. This prefab provides the Oculus stereo rendering and head tracking required for Gear VR support. Let's take a look at how it is constructed.

In the Hierarchy pane, locate the *OVRCameraRig* object, and expand it by clicking the down arrow icon to the left of the name. The camera rig contains a child object, *TrackingSpace*. Expand that, and you'll see four children: *LeftEyeAnchor*, *CenterEyeAnchor*, *RightEyeAnchor*, and *TrackerAnchor*. The center anchor is the key: it contains the camera setup for the application, which is used by the built-in Unity VR support to render the view from the left and right eyes, respectively. The Unity engine copies the camera parameters from the center anchor's camera to the left and right cameras it uses internally to render the scene. You can see in the Inspector pane by selecting *CenterEyeAnchor* that it contains a camera component with values for projection, field of view, background (used to paint the scene's background color for each render cycle), and so on.

The *TrackerAnchor* is there so that the application can always know the current position and orientation of the camera. This is useful in a variety of scenarios. Perhaps we want to have objects that are always placed relative to the camera at a certain distance; in this way we can properly place them whenever the camera moves. Or maybe we are creating a networked multiplayer game. For that, it is crucial to know where each player is and in which direction he is looking. The left and right anchors are there for completeness, so that we always have the individual position and orientation of the left and right cameras if we need that information (more on this momentarily).

To get a feel for how the anchor objects are implemented, let's look at some Unity script code. In the Hierarchy pane, select the object *OVRCameraRig* again. You will see that it contains a few script components. We want to look at the properties for the component labeled *OVR Camera Rig (Script)*. Its Script property has the value *OVRCameraRig*. Double-click on that value and MonoDevelop, Unity's code editor for C# programmers, will open the source file *OVRCameraRig.cs* from the project sources.

In the MonoDevelop source code window, scroll through or search until you find the definition of the method Update(), shown here:

```
private void Update()
{
    EnsureGameObjectIntegrity();

    if (!Application.isPlaying)
        return;

    UpdateAnchors();

#if UNITY_ANDROID && !UNITY_EDITOR

    if (!correctedTrackingSpace)
```

```
    {
        //HACK: Unity 5.1.1p3 double-counts the head model on
        //Android. Subtract it off in the reference frame.

        var headModel = new Vector3(0f,
            OVRManager.profile.eyeHeight - OVRManager.profile.neckHeight,
            OVRManager.profile.eyeDepth);
        var eyePos = -headModel + centerEyeAnchor.localRotation * headModel;

        if ((eyePos - centerEyeAnchor.localPosition).magnitude > 0.01f)
        {
            trackingSpace.localPosition =
                trackingSpace.localPosition -
                2f * (trackingSpace.localRotation * headModel);
            correctedTrackingSpace = true;
        }
    }
#endif
    }
```

The first few lines of this method behave exactly as described in Chapter 3. For a fully detailed description of that code, please refer back to "Walking Through the Code" on page 44.

The basic steps are:

1. The camera rig's Update() method first calls a helper, EnsureGameObjectInteg rity(), to make sure that the scene contains all of the required objects, that is the objects defined in the *OVRCameraRig* prefab.
2. After a check to see whether the application is actually running—it may not be, either because it hasn't been set into run mode yet or because the object is being viewed in the Unity editor and not in play mode—we do some real work.
3. We need to position and orient the anchor objects based on where the Oculus Rift HMD is looking. This is done in the method UpdateAnchors().
4. After the basic update logic, there is conditional code to handle Android-specific behavior in the Unity runtime; it's essentially a workaround to a bug in the Unity engine for Android.

That's it—we're now up and running on Gear VR.

Handling Touchpad Events

Virtual reality isn't only about rendering and camera tracking. We also need to process user input. The Gear VR comes with the touchpad, a great input device built into the side of the HMD. This is going to be our main source of input. Let's get a feel for how to use it.

Create a new Unity project, and call it *UnityGearVRInput*. As you did for the first example, import the Oculus Utilities package into the new project. In the Project pane, open the folder *Assets/OVR/Scenes* and double-click the scene named *Room*.

This loads a very simple scene, just a gray box that will be the inside of the room. This example uses the touchpad to rotate the camera within the room. You should be able to see it in the Game view, located at the bottom left of the Unity interface, as highlighted by the red circle in Figure 4-6.

In the Hierarchy pane you should see several objects: an object named *OVRPlayerController*, six cubes, and a directional light. *OVRPlayerController* is another SDK prefab; this one contains a camera rig, like the previous example, but it uses touchpad input instead of head tracking to move the camera. If you expand the prefab by clicking on the down arrow icon you will see the object's contents, including the camera rig and several script components, in the Inspector pane.

Now let's run the example. As before, you need to set up your build settings. Select Android in the platforms list and then press the Switch Platform button. Click Add Current to add the room sample to the build. Configure your other settings as you did earlier—then click the Player Settings, then click the Virtual Reality Supported, Bundle Identifier, and Minimum API Level settings. Also, remember to copy the signature file for your device. Once this is all done, you should be able to build and run the sample.

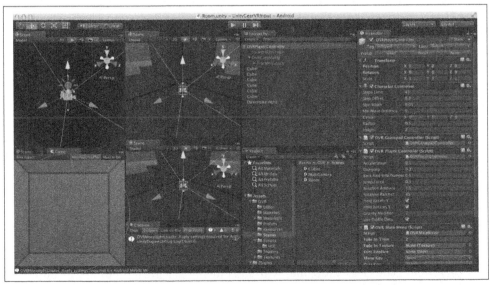

Figure 4-6. Room scene Game view—Gear VR input example

Assuming you were successful, you will be inside a gray box. Swipe the touchpad to rotate your view within the box. Now let's look at the code. Select the object *OVR-*

PlayerController in the Hierarchy pane. You'll see its properties in the Inspector pane, including several scripts. Find the script named *OVR Player Controller (Script)*, and double-click the value for its Script property. This will open the source file *OVR-PlayerController.cs* in MonoDevelop.

The script's Update() method is quite involved. We are mostly concerned with a helper method, UpdateMovement(). This method, which also works on the desktop, uses the current mouse *X* position to calculate a rotation about the *Y* (up) axis for the camera. Scroll to or search for that method and, within it, the lines of code that check for mouse input (at or near line 296):

```
//#if !UNITY_ANDROID || UNITY_EDITOR
        if (!SkipMouseRotation)
            euler.y += Input.GetAxis("Mouse X") * rotateInfluence * 3.25f;
//#endif
```

We can use the same mouse-based approach to handle touchpad input, because the Oculus Utilities package automatically converts touchpad input to mouse input:

- Forward/back swipes on the touchpad are converted to mouse movement in *X*.
- Up/down swipes are converted to mouse movement in *Y*.
- Taps on the touchpad are converted to mouse button presses, with mouse button code 0.
- Taps on the back button next to the touchpad are converted to mouse button presses, with mouse button code 1.

Trackpad Hack

Note the lines in italics in the preceding code fragment. I had to hack the source to comment out the *#ifdef* and *#endif* statements to get the trackpad to work on the Gear VR, as for some unknown reason Android mouse handling was disabled. This hack does the trick.

The mouse *X* and *Y* values are obtained by calling Input.GetAxis(), a function that is built into the Unity input system. The variable euler is a *euler angle*; that is, an *x,y,z* triple that represents rotation about each individual axis. The method continues for a while, potentially also getting input from a gamepad controller, but we are not using one in this example. The last line in the method converts the computed euler value to a quaternion and saves it into the player controller's transform, thereby rotating the controller, which ultimately results in the rotation of its descendant camera rig:

```
transform.rotation=Quaternion.Euler(euler);
```

Deploying Applications for Gear VR

So, you've developed and tested your application, and it's working. Now you want to publish it to the Oculus Store for the world to experience. How do you do that?

A full treatment of the topic is out of scope for this book, but we'll go through the basics. First, you need to sign your application. You must replace the temporary Oculus signature file used in development with a valid Android application signature file. The Android SDK (*http://bit.ly/android-signing-apps*) contains information on how to do this. Unity has integrated support for signing your application, which can be found at Edit → Project Settings → Player → Publishing Options. Use that interface to insert a newly created Android keystore generated by the Android SDK.

Once you have generated an Android package file *.apk* with a valid signature, you can submit it to the Oculus Store. This is a bit of a process, involving packaging image files in known directories, writing application manifests, exchanging files via Dropbox and emailing back and forth with the Oculus Store online service and, presumably, humans on the other end making the final approvals.

Full instructions for publishing to the Oculus Store can be found online (*http://bit.ly/oculus-publish*).

Chapter Summary

In this chapter, we learned how to develop applications for the Gear VR, Samsung's revolutionary mobile VR headset powered by Oculus technology. We explored the current editions of the hardware and supported phones, and took a quick look at the wonderfully designed user interface known as the Oculus Store.

Unity3D comes with excellent support for developing Gear VR applications. We created sample projects to render in stereo, track HMD motion, and use the touchpad for input.

This chapter also took a quick look at the full cycle of developing, testing, debugging, and deploying for Gear VR, including using the Android SDK, the Oculus Mobile SDK, the Oculus Utilities for Unity package, and the Oculus code signing tool, and submitting applications to the Oculus Store.

While the material covered in this chapter is simple in concept, the devil is in the details. Developing for Android is no picnic. Unity3D is powerful but takes some getting used to, and the additional quirks in dealing with Gear VR and Oculus Store deployment make everything that much more...*interesting*. But hopefully you will find that it's worth the trouble. The Gear VR is a great device, and a major step on the road to consumer-grade, mass-market virtual reality.

CHAPTER 5

WebVR: Browser-Based Virtual Reality in HTML5

And now for something completely different.

In previous chapters we saw how to use native platform SDKs to create virtual reality applications with great graphics, high performance, and a sense of presence. If we are developing a single-user experience for a specific desktop or mobile platform, and don't mind that it requires an app download and install, then this approach may be all that we ever need.

But many of us creating VR would prefer to build web applications. Why? Because integrating VR with the Web offers the following advantages over native applications:

Instant access
> No download and app install required; just type a URL or click on a hyperlink to launch virtual reality experiences.

Easy integration of web data
> Data from sources like Wikipedia, YouTube, and social networks can easily be incorporated, and there are open APIs to thousands of web services.

Cross-platform compatibility
> HTML5 runs on all desktop and mobile devices. On mobile platforms, HTML5 code can either be delivered via browsers or embedded in apps.

Faster, cheaper development
> HTML5 and JavaScript are arguably the easiest cross-platform system for creating apps ever devised, and we can use our choice of open source development tools, most of which are free of charge.

Easier deployment

> The cloud is set up to deliver web applications, and updates just happen without having to go through app stores.

There is such a strong belief in this idea that work is already taking place to make it happen. The latest generation of web browsers include support for virtual reality, using new APIs and related technologies dubbed "WebVR."

While WebVR is in its early stages, still only running in developer builds of browsers, it is already showing promising results. Figure 5-1 shows a screenshot of a demo created by Brandon Jones of Google: a version of id Software's *Quake 3*, ported to WebGL and running in the browser. Note the Oculus distortion: this version renders to an Oculus Rift and tracks head movements to update the camera, using the WebVR API.

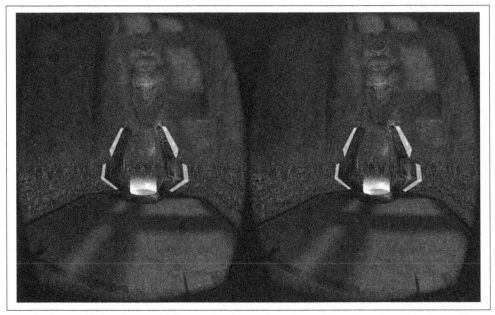

Figure 5-1. Quake 3 (http://bit.ly/quake3-demo) WebVR demo, developed by Brandon Jones of Google

This chapter explores how to develop using WebVR. We'll study the details of the API currently available in nightly developer builds of Firefox and Chrome. Then we will take a peek at rendering 3D in the browser with WebGL using the popular Three.js library, and survey open source tools for putting together VR applications for the Web. But first, let's look at how this exciting new development in web browser technology came to be.

The Story of WebVR

The roots of WebVR can be traced to the spring of 2014. In the wake of the historic acquisition of Oculus VR by Facebook, Mozilla engineer Vlad Vukićević and his colleague, VR researcher Josh Carpenter, began work to add Oculus Rift support to Firefox. There had been previous attempts to integrate the Rift with browsers as far back as the DK1, using either webSockets or browser plugins to communicate with the head-tracking IMU hardware. But the performance of these solutions was relatively slow, resulting in motion lag and the associated queasiness.

Vukićević and Carpenter decided to see how far they could get with a native implementation built into the browser, one free of the performance issues that came with plugins. By summer, Mozilla had released a first, experimental version of the code in a developer-only build of Firefox available for download on Vlad's personal blog (*http://bit.ly/vr-first-steps*), along with a few pieces of example content.

In June 2014, just prior to the first public release, the Mozilla team presented their work at the San Francisco WebGL Developers Meetup, an 800-strong group that meets to discuss 3D rendering in browsers. Josh Carpenter came to present, and brought along Brandon Jones, an engineer on the Chrome team, to demo his own VR prototype. It turned out the two teams had already been collaborating to create a common API between the two browsers, and not two months after beginning their projects, they had achieved it: using this new API, programmers could write their VR code once and run it in both browsers. At that moment, WebVR was born.

Since that June 2014 meeting, there has been a flurry of activity, including revisions to the API, showcase websites, interface design research; and local meetup groups and whole websites devoted to learning about WebVR. For more information, Appendix A contains a list of WebVR resources.

The Web and the Power of Collaboration

The collaboration between Mozilla and Google on WebVR is a testament to the power of web standards and open community development. The Mozilla team were the prime movers, and could have run with their own implementation a long time before bringing in other browser makers, but instead they decided to include Google in the discussion early on. This provided instant validation of the idea and also gave outside developers a high level of confidence that they could build cross-browser VR applications. This kind of collaboration is something you would never see with a closed-system VR platform.

Note that as of this writing, WebVR is not a *standard*. Rather, it is a set of extensions built into the two most popular browsers. But that's OK; this actually follows a typical pattern for modern browser development, where new capabilities are added as experimental features first, and then standardized after the features have been evaluated and tested by developers. Someday, we could see the WebVR API added as a W3C recommendation and becoming a true standard.

The WebVR API

Browsers already have the capability to do stunning real-time 3D rendering using WebGL, the API standard for rendering 3D graphics using JavaScript. So, as it turns out—and this is not to take anything away from the great efforts of the engineers involved—adding VR support to browsers actually required very few modifications. The WebVR API comprises these key browser innovations:

Discovering/connecting to VR devices
> The browser provides an API for the developer to discover and connect to the VR device(s) attached to the computer.

VR fullscreen mode
> Web browsers already have a fullscreen mode to support game development. VR fullscreen mode extends this to automatically put the VR device, such as a Rift, into the correct video driver mode on the computer. It also performs the Oculus-style barrel distortion in native code, so the programmers don't have to implement it in their applications.

Head tracking
> A new JavaScript API tracks head position and orientation so that we can adjust the camera each frame before we render.

With these three features, a well-designed JavaScript application can use WebGL to render virtual reality scenes. Let's have a look at how to use them.

Supported Browsers and Devices

WebVR is currently implemented in development builds of Firefox and Chrome. To try them out, download Firefox Nightly (*http://mozvr.com/downloads/*) or the Chromium WebVR build (*http://bit.ly/webvr-builds*).

These are still experimental builds, but the hope is that someday WebVR features will make it into retail versions of the browsers. There are a few serious limitations—for example, browsers have historically throttled refresh rates at 60 frames per second, whereas good VR requires 75–90 FPS to provide convincing immersion. In addition, the installation process is still fairly manual, as it requires installing the Oculus SDK separately.

WebVR, Mobile Browsers, and Google Cardboard

Note that the API and techniques described in this chapter are not for use with Google's *Cardboard VR*. Cardboard is a specification for rendering 3D scenes with a mobile phone dropped into an inexpensive side-by-side head-mounted stereo viewer, using the phone's IMU to track head movements. It is possible to build Cardboard apps using a mobile browser; we'll cover this, along with general Cardboard development topics, in the next chapter.

Querying for VR Devices

The first thing a WebVR application needs to do is query the browser for which VR devices are connected to the computer. WebVR currently supports Oculus DK1 and DK2 devices, but eventually it could support others; also, multiple VR devices may be connected to the computer at once. Example 5-1 shows how to use the browser function `getVRDevices()` to get a list of connected devices.

About the JavaScript Language

The examples in this chapter assume basic familiarity with Java-Script. See "Programming Languages" on page 139 if you don't have any experience with this language.

Example 5-1. Querying for VR devices

```
myVRApp.prototype.queryVRDevices = function() {

    // Polyfill - hide FF/WebKit differences
    var getVRDevices = navigator.mozGetVRDevices /* FF */ ||
                       navigator.getVRDevices; /* WebKit */

    if (!getVRDevices) {
        // Handle error here, via either throwing an exception or
        // calling an error callback
    }

    var self = this;
    getVRDevices().then( gotVRDevices );
    function gotVRDevices( devices ) {
        // Look for HMDVRDevice (display) first
        var vrHMD;
        var error;
        for ( var i = 0; i < devices.length; ++i ) {
            if ( devices[i] instanceof HMDVRDevice ) {
                vrHMD = devices[i];
                self._vrHMD = vrHMD;
                if ( vrHMD.getEyeParameters ) {
                    self.left = vrHMD.getEyeParameters( "left" );
```

```
            self.right = vrHMD.getEyeParameters( "right" );
        }
        self.leftEyeTranslation = vrHMD.getEyeTranslation( "left" );
        self.rightEyeTranslation = vrHMD.getEyeTranslation( "right" );
        self.leftEyeFOV = vrHMD.getRecommendedEyeFieldOfView( "left" );
        self.rightEyeFOV = vrHMD.getRecommendedEyeFieldOfView( "right" );
        break; // We keep the first we encounter
    }
}

// Now look for PositionSensorVRDevice (head tracking)
var vrInput;
var error;
for ( var i = 0; i < devices.length; ++i ) {
    if ( devices[i] instanceof PositionSensorVRDevice ) {
        vrInput = devices[i]
        self._vrInput = vrInput;
        break; // We keep the first we encounter
    }
}

    }
}
```

In the examples in this section, we have created a JavaScript class named myVRApp. myVRApp defines the method queryVRDevices() to do the query. First, we need to find the correct version of the query function in a cross-browser way. For both Firefox and Chrome, this function is a method on the navigator object; but Firefox names it moz GetVRDevices(), while the Chrome name is getVRDevices(). Note that this is the only place in WebVR where we need conditional code based on which browser is running; from here, the API is identical across browsers.

We save the correct version of the function into a local variable, getVRDevices, and use that to make the query. Functions like this use JavaScript *promises*, objects that have a then() method used to supply a callback function. The callback function, gotVRDevices(), iterates through the list of connected VR devices, looking for two kinds of devices. HMDVRDevice objects represent the connected display hardware, and PositionSensorVRDevice objects represent the head-tracking hardware. (While the Oculus Rift has those two types of hardware integrated into a single device, that may not be the case with all VR hardware in the future, so the API designers thought it best to separate the two types in order to keep the design general enough for future use.) If found, the devices are tucked away into the object's _vrHMD and _vrInput properties for use in the application.

Note the line of code near the beginning of the method that checks whether getVR Devices is non-null:

```
if (!getVRDevices) {
```

This test is important; it's our way of determining whether the WebVR API exists at all. This allows us to write robust code that also works in browsers that don't support WebVR (for example, by reporting to the user that the application requires a WebVR-enabled browser).

Setting Up VR Fullscreen Mode

VR applications must run fullscreen to create a feeling of immersion. Web browsers have supported fullscreen mode for several years in order to run video games, but VR fullscreen requires additional treatment: the browser may have to use special display modes, depending on the VR hardware, and it may also need to perform additional visual processing, such as Oculus Rift barrel distortion. For WebVR, the browser method to go into fullscreen mode has been extended so that we can pass in the HMDVRDevice obtained from getVRDevices() The following code shows how this is done.

```
myVRApp.prototype.goFullScreen = function() {

    var vrHMD = this._vrHMD;

    // this._canvas is an HTML5 canvas element
    var canvas = this._canvas;

    // Polyfill - hide FF/Webkit differences
    function requestFullScreen() {
        if ( canvas.mozRequestFullScreen ) {
         canvas.mozRequestFullScreen( { vrDisplay: vrHMD } );
        } else {
         canvas.webkitRequestFullscreen( { vrDisplay: vrHMD } );
      }
    }

requestFullScreen();
}
```

The application object defines a helper, goFullScreen(), that hides the details, but there is actually not that much to it. We just need to ask the browser to put the graphics window into VR fullscreen mode using the HMD. The graphics window in this case is an HTML5 canvas, the one used to render the application with WebGL. Previously, during initialization, we saved the WebGL canvas in the _canvas property of the object. Now, we call a method of the canvas to go into fullscreen mode. This is another one of those places where different browsers use a different method name (unfortunate, but this seems to be a fairly common practice for somewhat new features like fullscreen mode): mozRequestFullScreen() for Firefox, and web kitRequestFullScreen() for Chrome. Though the method names are different, their signatures are the same. We pass the HMD device to this method, indicating that we want VR fullscreen mode instead of regular fullscreen mode.

Head Tracking

The final piece of the WebVR API implements head tracking. We need to be able to obtain an accurate position and orientation from the device, and reflect that in the current position and orientation of the camera at all times.

The following code shows WebVR head tracking in action. Our application defines a method, update(), that is called each time it is ready to render the scene. update() uses the head-tracking device that the application saved into the property _vrInput when it originally queried for VR devices. The head-tracking device has a method, getState(), that returns an object with the current position and orientation. Those values, if present, are copied into the position and orientation of the camera being used to render the scene:

```
myVRApp.prototype.update = function() {

    var vrInput = this._vrInput;
    var vrState = vrInput.getState();

    if ( !vrState ) {
        return;
    }

    // Update the camera's position and orientation
    if ( vrState.position !== null ) {
        this.setCameraPosition( vrState.position );
    }

    if ( vrState.orientation !== null ) {
        this.setCameraOrientation( vrState.orientation );
    }

}
```

These are the basics of the WebVR API. In the next section, we'll put them into practice in the context of a full application.

Creating a WebVR Application

Now that we have a sense of how the API works, let's shift gears and look at how to put WebVR applications together. Web applications are different beasts from native desktop and mobile apps, and developing for HTML5 comes with its own set of challenges and trade-offs. The Web offers many choices in open source tools and libraries, but most of the tools aren't as polished as systems like Unity3D and Unreal. We have cross-platform development capability, but we still need to be mindful about the differences between browsers; and while it's easy to get web applications online, deploying them professionally can be a black art.

In this section we will build a full, though quite simple, WebVR application to illustrate the issues. We will look at how to put together a web "page" that is the WebVR app; how to create and render 3D scenes using Three.js, a popular JavaScript library for programming WebGL; how to use Three.js objects that implement Oculus Rift stereoscopic rendering and head tracking; and finally, how to implement an HTML5-based user interface suitable for launching into VR fullscreen mode. Let's do it.

Three.js: A JavaScript 3D Engine

As WebVR developers, we'll need to do 3D rendering. The API of choice for rendering 3D in a web browser is WebGL. WebGL runs in all browsers and on all platforms and devices. It allows us access to the full capabilities of the graphics processing unit to create beautiful real-time 3D renderings and animations in web pages for all types of applications, and it's perfectly suited to rendering virtual reality. But to do anything more than the most basic tasks using the API out of the box requires serious effort and literally hundreds of lines of code. This is not a recipe for rapidly building applications in the modern world. So, unless you feel like creating a 3D game engine from scratch, you will probably want to find a library to help ease the burden.

While there are many choices for getting started with WebGL development, the undisputed leader in this category is Three.js (*http://threejs.org/*). Three.js provides an easy, intuitive set of objects that are commonly found in 3D graphics. It is fast, using many best-practice graphics engine techniques. It is powerful, with several built-in object types and handy utilities. It is open source, hosted on GitHub (*http://bit.ly/threejs-3d*), and well maintained, with several authors contributing to it.

Three.js has become a de facto choice for WebGL development. Most of the great WebGL content you can view online has been built with it, and there are several rich and highly innovative works live on the Web today. The WebVR team at Mozilla developed a set of objects for extending Three.js with VR capability and contributed them to the project, and now many developers are using those extensions to create the new generation of Three.js applications for WebVR.

A Full Example

Before we dig into the code, let's run the example depicted in Figure 5-2. Here we see the Chromium browser running windowed, displaying the stereo rendering for a cube texture-mapped with the WebVR logo.

If you have your Oculus Rift attached to the computer, you can tilt the headset and you will see the cube move around the screen. (Actually, the camera is moving in response to the changes in the headset's orientation.)

Now, click the Start VR Mode button. This will put the browser in fullscreen mode. It's time to put on your Rift and look around. You should now be immersed in the experience. And there it is: welcome to WebVR!

Setting up the project

To look through the code, you can clone the repository from GitHub (*https://github.com/tparisi/WebVR*).

Running Web Examples on Your Local Machine

If you plan to run this and other web examples from your local machine, you will need to run them using a web server.

I run a local version of a standard LAMP stack on my MacBook, but all you really need is the "A" part of LAMP (i.e., a web server such as Apache). If you have Python installed, another option is the `SimpleHTTPServer` module, which you can run by going to the root of the examples directory and typing:

```
python -m SimpleHTTPServer
```

Then point your web browser at *http://localhost:8000/*. There is a great tech tip on this feature on the *Linux Journal (http://bit.ly/httpserver-py)* website.

The web page

All web applications start with a web page, and WebVR apps are no exception. The following listing shows the HTML5 markup for the web page. After a bit of header information that includes the title and some embedded CSS to style the Start VR Mode button and 3D canvas, we see the body of the page. It's pretty simple, containing just two elements: an element named `button` for the button, and one named `container` that will contain a WebGL canvas for drawing. We will initialize the 3D contents of `container` in a moment, using JavaScript. This is it for the page markup:

```
<html>
<head>
<meta http-equiv="Content-Type" content="text/html; charset=UTF-8">
<title>WebVR &mdash; Oculus Rift Three.js Cube</title>
      <style>

            .button {
                position: absolute;
                bottom: 20px;
                right: 20px;
                padding: 8px;
                color: #FFF;
                background-color: #555;
                z-index:1;
```

```
        }

        #container {
            position:absolute;
            left:0;
            top:0;
            width:100%;
            height:100%;
        }

    </style>

</head>
<body>

    <div class="button">Start VR Mode</div>
    <div id="container"></div>

</body>
```

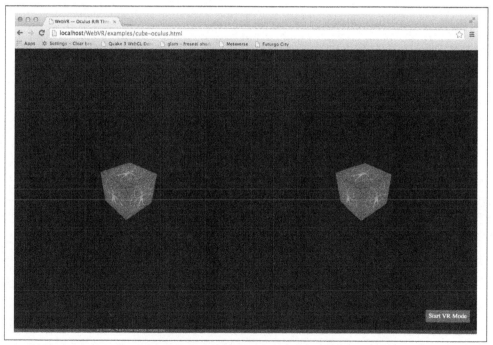

Figure 5-2. A simple WebVR example running in the Chromium WebVR-enabled build:
WebVR logo via Pixabay (http://bit.ly/pixabay-webvr)

The JavaScript code

The next few lines on the page are script elements that include JavaScript code for
various web libraries. The important ones here are the script elements for Three.js

and the two Three.js extensions for WebVR, the classes `THREE.VREffect` and `THREE.VRControls`. These extensions were developed by Diego Marcos of Mozilla and contributed to the Three.js repository on GitHub. Like many Three.js extensions, they are not built into the main build of Three.js, but they are included in the examples that come with the project:

```
<script src="../libs/jquery-1.9.1/jquery-1.9.1.js"></script>
<script src="../libs/three.js.r68/three.js"></script>
<script src="../libs/three.js.r68/effects/VREffect.js"></script>
<script src="../libs/three.js.r68/controls/VRControls.js"></script>
<script src="../libs/requestAnimationFrame/RequestAnimationFrame.js"></script>
```

Following these, we have a script element with several lines of JavaScript defined inline, shown in Example 5-3. This is the code for the application. It starts with the main program, a jQuery callback function that will be called once the page is loaded and ready. The function calls several helper functions, which we will go through in detail.

Example 5-3. The main JavaScript program

```
<script type="text/javascript">
    var container = null,
    renderer = null,
    effect = null,
    controls = null,
    scene = null,
    camera = null,
    cube = null;

    $(document).ready(function() {
        // Set up Three.js
        initThreeJS();

        // Set up VR rendering
        initVREffect();

        // Create the scene content
        initScene();

        // Set up VR camera controls
        initVRControls();

        // Set the viewport size and aspect ratio
        refreshSize();

        // Run the run loop
        requestAnimationFrame(run);
    });
```

First, we have to initialize our use of the Three.js library. Let's look at the code for this:

```
function initThreeJS() {
    container = document.getElementById("container");
    // Create the Three.js renderer and attach it to our canvas
    renderer = new THREE.WebGLRenderer( { antialias: true } );

    // Set the viewport size
    container.appendChild(renderer.domElement);

    window.addEventListener( 'resize', refreshSize, false );

}
```

We ask Three.js to create a new renderer object, asking it to render in WebGL using antialiasing. Antialiasing is a rendering technique that eliminates jagged lines. It's not turned on by default, so we must specify this by passing the antialias property to the constructor. Under the covers, the Three.js renderer object creates a DOM Canvas element, which is required for rendering WebGL. We add the canvas to our page, and we are now ready to render graphics. As a final flourish we add a resize handler, so that when the window is resized the Three.js renderer object is, too. Three.js initialization is now complete.

Next, we call the helper function initVREffect() to set up stereo rendering and fullscreen mode handling:

```
function initVREffect() {
    // Set up Oculus renderer
    effect = new THREE.VREffect(renderer, function(err) {
        if (err) {
            console.log("Error creating VREffect: ", err);
        }
        else {
            console.log("Created VREffect: ", effect);
        }
    });

    // Set up fullscreen mode handling
    var fullScreenButton = document.querySelector( '.button' );
    fullScreenButton.onclick = function() {
        effect.setFullScreen(true);
    };
}
```

initVREffect() creates an instance of THREE.VREffect, which will be used in our run loop to render the scene in stereo from two cameras. The function also sets up fullscreen mode by adding a callback to the button object defined in the markup. The callback calls the effect's setFullScreen() method to go into fullscreen mode when the button is clicked.

Now, we need to create the 3D content that we will render in the scene. With Three.js, we can create content by loading models in a variety of 3D formats, such as Wavefront OBJ and COLLADA, or we can create it by writing code. We'll do the latter, as shown here:

```
function initScene() {
    // Create a new Three.js scene
    scene = new THREE.Scene();

    // Add a camera so we can view the scene
    // Note that this camera's FOV is ignored in favor of the
    // Oculus-supplied FOV for each used inside VREffect.
    // See VREffect.js h/t Michael Blix
    camera = new THREE.PerspectiveCamera( 90,
      window.innerWidth / window.innerHeight, 1, 4000 );
    scene.add(camera);

    // Create a texture-mapped cube and add it to the scene
    // First, create the texture map
    var mapUrl = "../images/webvr-logo-512.jpeg";
    var map = THREE.ImageUtils.loadTexture(mapUrl);

    // Now, create a Basic material; pass in the map
    var material = new THREE.MeshBasicMaterial({ map: map });

    // Create the cube geometry
    var geometry = new THREE.BoxGeometry(2, 2, 2);

    // And put the geometry and material together into a mesh
    cube = new THREE.Mesh(geometry, material);

    // Move the mesh back from the camera and tilt it toward the viewer
    cube.position.z = -6;
    cube.rotation.x = Math.PI / 5;
    cube.rotation.y = Math.PI / 5;

    // Finally, add the mesh to our scene
    scene.add( cube );

}
```

Three.js has a simple, easy-to-use paradigm for creating graphics. The scene consists of a hierarchy of objects. At the root is a THREE.Scene, and each object is added as a child of that scene, or a descendant thereof. This particular scene consists of just the cube and a camera from which to view it. We create the camera first, a THREE.PerspectiveCamera. The parameters to the camera's constructor are field of view, aspect ratio, and the distance from the camera to the front and back clipping planes. Under the covers, the VREffect object used by WebVR will ignore the field of view, using instead a set of values provided in the HMDVRDevice device we discovered when we initialized the VREffect.

The remainder of the scene-creation code concerns building the cube. The cube object is a Three.js mesh, of type THREE.Mesh. To create a mesh, we need a piece of geometry and a material. The geometry is of type THREE.BoxGeometry, and the material is a THREE.MeshBasicMaterial: that is, an unlit object, which in this case has a texture map. We supply the texture map as the map property to the material's constructor. After we create the mesh, we move it back a little bit from the camera—which is positioned at the origin by default—and rotate it a bit around the *x*- and *y*-axes so that we can see it's a real 3D object. We add it to the scene as a child, and with that, we have a visual scene ready to render. We're almost there!

The last major piece of VR support is to set up head tracking. With Three.js we do this by creating a *camera controller*—that is, an object that changes the position and orientation of the camera based on user input. For non-VR applications, Three.js comes with first-person controllers, orbit controllers, and other ways to move the camera based on mouse and keyboard input. For WebVR, we need a controller that uses the WebVR API for head tracking. Diego's WebVR extension comes with a class, THREE.VRControls, for this purpose. As we can see from the following code listing, it's really only one line of code to set up, though in this example we are also supplying an error handler for the case when the app can't create the controller for some reason (e.g., the browser is not VR-ready):

```
function initVRControls() {

    // Set up VR camera controls
    controls = new THREE.VRControls(camera, function(err) {
        if (err) {
            console.log("Error creating VRControls: ", err);
        }
        else {
            console.log("Created VRControls: ", controls);
        }
    });
}
```

For the final setup step, we want to make sure that the Three.js rendering viewport is sized correctly. We define a resize handler function, refreshSize(), that will be called any time the window is resized. We'll use this same function to calculate the viewport size the first time through. See the lines in italics:

```
function refreshSize ( ) {
    var fullWidth = document.body.clientWidth,
        fullHeight = document.body.clientHeight,
        canvasWidth,
        canvasHeight,
        aspectWidth;
    if ( effect && effect.isFullScreen ) {
        canvasWidth = effect.left.renderRect.width +
            effect.right.renderRect.width;
```

```
            canvasHeight = Math.max( effect.left.renderRect.height,
                effect.right.renderRect.height );
            aspectWidth = canvasWidth / 2;
        }
        else {
            var ratio = window.devicePixelRatio || 1;
            canvasWidth = fullWidth * ratio;
            canvasHeight = fullHeight * ratio;
            aspectWidth = canvasWidth;
        }
        renderer.domElement.style.width = fullWidth + "px";
        renderer.domElement.style.height = fullHeight + "px";
        renderer.domElement.width = canvasWidth;
        renderer.domElement.height = canvasHeight;
        renderer.setViewport( 0, 0, canvasWidth, canvasHeight );
        camera.aspect = aspectWidth / canvasHeight;
        camera.updateProjectionMatrix( );
    }
```

refreshSize() goes through several lines of DOM code to calculate the actual size of
the canvas based on whether we are running fullscreen or windowed mode. Once we
have those values, we set the size of the Three.js viewport, and also reset the camera's
projection matrix in case the window's aspect ratio (width/height) has changed.

That's it for setup and initialization. The only thing left is to implement the *run loop*,
which is the heart of our application. The run loop drives continuous animation
and rendering of 3D scenes, by handing the browser a callback function that it will
call every time it is ready to render the contents of the page again. Let's walk through
the listing:

```
var duration = 10000; // ms
function animate(deltat) {
    var fract = deltat / duration;
    var angle = Math.PI * 2 * fract;
    cube.rotation.y += angle;
}

var lastTime = 0;
function run(time) {
    requestAnimationFrame(run);
    var dt = time - lastTime;
    lastTime = time;
    // Render the scene
    effect.render( scene, camera );

    // Update the VR camera controls
    controls.update();

    // Spin the cube for next frame
    animate(dt);
}
```

The helper function `animate()` is responsible for animating the scene by rotating the cube a little about the *y*-axis in each frame. It does this by calculating how much to add to the *y* rotation as a function of time. Each time through, we ask the browser for the current time (in milliseconds) and subtract a previously saved value to obtain `deltat`; `deltat` is then divided by our duration value—in this case, 10 seconds—to obtain a fractional amount, and the fraction is used to calculate `angle`, a rotation that is a fraction of 2 * pi radians (or 360 degrees).

But you may be wondering how `animate()` gets called. Modern browsers support a function, `requestAnimationFrame()`, that an application can use to request the browser to call it when it's ready to redraw the page. We pass our `run()` function to that, and thus we have our run loop. Every time through the run loop, `run()` performs the following actions:

1. Render the scene using the `THREE.VREffect` object, which renders in stereo suitable for WebVR.
2. Update the `THREE.VRControls` object, which polls the connected WebVR devices for the latest position and updates the main camera.
3. Call `animate()` to drive the animation of the rotating cube.

And that's it. This example is contrived, sure, but it shows the basics of building an end-to-end WebVR application. With the tools covered in the next section, we can go far beyond spinning cubes; we can create full VR applications with high production values and awesome performance.

If you are curious about the inner workings of Mozilla's WebVR extensions to Three.js, you can look through the code in the latest repository on GitHub (*https:// github.com/mrdoob/three.js/*). Also, the source files for the WebVR extensions are included in the GitHub project (*https://github.com/tparisi/WebVR*) for this example.

Tools and Techniques for Creating Web VR

Now that we have seen how to build a basic WebVR application using the new browser APIs and the Three.js library, it's time to take a step back. While Three.js is a great, easy way to get started, it is by no means our only way to create and deploy WebVR. Let's take a quick tour of the tools and frameworks at our disposal.

WebVR Engines and Development Tools

Over the last few years, several tools have emerged to create 3D content and applications for the Web using WebGL. Unlike tools like Unity3D and Unreal, these products are web applications; there is no need to download packaged software. Developers use a web-based interface to create or import art, and then add behaviors, scripts, and interaction, all within a browser. Several such tools have been enhanced recently to support virtual reality via WebVR, including:

PlayCanvas (http://www.playcanvas.com/)
London-based PlayCanvas has developed a rich 3D engine and cloud-based authoring tool. The authoring tool features real-time collaborative scene editing to support team development; GitHub and Bitbucket integration; and one-button publishing to social media networks. The PlayCanvas engine is open source and can be downloaded from GitHub (*https://github.com/playcanvas*).

One PlayCanvas developer has built an Oculus-enabled version of *AfterGlow*, a downhill ski racing game created to promote Philips' Ambilight lighting product (see *http://afterglowskigame.com*). There is also a PlayCanvas add-in on GitHub (*https://github.com/playcanvas/oculus-vr*). Figure 5-3 shows a screenshot of the PlayCanvas development environment.

Goo Create (http://www.gootechnologies.com/)
Goo is oriented toward digital marketing, but the engine boasts a list of traditional game engine features. The company is building apps and experiences both for the Oculus and more lightweight mobile systems such as Moggles (*http://moggles.com*).

Goo Create now features a VR camera script in the asset library; this can be dragged and dropped inside the viewport on a camera and voilá—instant VR.

Verold Studio (http://www.verold.com)
Verold Studio is a lightweight publishing platform for 3D interactive content developed by Toronto-based Verold, Inc. It is a no-plugin, extensible system with a simple JavaScript API, so that hobbyists, students, educators, visual communication specialists, and web marketers can integrate 3D animated content easily into their web properties. Verold customers are now moving their 3D creations into VR, including in education, architecture, and product design. Mozilla is also using it to build out its MozVR showcase site, described in "WebVR and the Future of Web Browsing" on page 83.

The tools surveyed above are very promising. However, they are still not that mature. Also, the usage fees and source code licensing for some of them are still in flux. Depending on your exact project needs and budget, your mileage may vary. Make sure to check the websites for the latest information on each tool.

Using Unity3D and Unreal for WebVR Development

If you are already developing desktop or mobile native and using Unity3D or Unreal, you probably don't want to learn another tool. The good news is that you don't have to: both Unity and Unreal have added WebGL export. As of this writing, the WebGL export feature in Unity is free to use, while the Unreal WebGL export is free to use but requires a royalty on games/apps sold. Consult the websites for these tools to get the most up-to-date licensing information.

Figure 5-3. PlayCanvas, a web-hosted game engine and development tool

Figure 5-4 shows the Unity3D WebGL exporter in action: a screenshot of the WebGL version of *Dead Trigger 2* (*http://bit.ly/dead-trigger-2*) by developer Madfinger Games.

For existing developers of native applications that want to try developing for the Web, this would seem like the perfect solution. But it's not without its issues. These export paths rely on a rather new technology called *Emscripten* (*http://bit.ly/emscripten*). Emscripten cross-compiles the actual code from a game engine like Unity to a low-level JavaScript called *asm.js* (*http://asmjs.org/*). The result is a game or experience with very high frame rate, comparable to a native game engine. But the cross-compiled engine code itself can consist of several megabytes of JavaScript code that has to get downloaded into the browser—before the game itself downloads. So expect to see lengthy load screens and progress bars before your VR experience comes over the wire. If this is acceptable, then no worries; if it's not, then maybe you want to look into using one of the engines discussed in the previous section.

Figure 5-4. WebGL version of Dead Trigger 2, using Unity3D WebGL exporter

Open Source Libraries and Frameworks

When it comes to JavaScript libraries for 3D development, Three.js isn't the only game in town. There are other great libraries worthy of a look, including:

Babylon.js (http://www.babylonjs.com/)
    A fully featured open source JavaScript library created by David Catuhe of Microsoft. BabylonJS has added a `BABYLON.WebVRCamera` object, which not only renders in stereo but also implements the camera controller, so it is like a combination of the two VR extensions to Three.js described earlier.

GLAM (http://www.glamjs.org/)
    A declarative language for 3D web content, which I designed. GLAM (for GL and Markup) combines the power of WebGL with a set of easy-to-use markup tags and style properties. To create 3D content, you define page elements, set their attributes, add event listeners, and define styles in CSS—just like authoring a web page. GLAM is intended for general web 3D development, but it also includes features for developing WebVR apps for the Oculus Rift and Cardboard VR. To get a taste of what authoring 3D markup might look like, refer to the following code:

```
<glam>
  <renderer type="rift"></renderer>
  <scene>
    <controller type="rift"></controller>
    <cube id="photocube"></cube>
```

```
      </scene>
    </glam>
```

The document defines a WebVR scene with a cube. Rather than writing dozens of lines of setup code in Three.js, you just author the content, and the GLAM library takes care of the rest.

SceneVR (http://www.scenevr.com/)

Another declarative language, created by Ben Nolan. SceneVR has been designed specifically for creating virtual reality scenes but is actually quite similar to GLAM. Ben and I are collaborating to create a unified tag set, though this work is preliminary.

WebVR and the Future of Web Browsing

WebVR has huge promise. The ability to access rich VR experiences without a download or install, and to author VR content using simple, affordable tools, could be revolutionary. But it is still very early, and there is going to be a lot of experimentation.

The user interface is a very interesting area for investigation. The design of web-connected VR applications raises interesting questions, such as: Once we create connected, fullscreen immersive VR experiences on the Web, how do we navigate between them? What is the equivalent of a bookmark? A cursor? The Back button? With these in mind, the Mozilla team, led by VR researcher Josh Carpenter, has launched MozVR (*http://www.mozvr.com/*), a combination showcase site and playground for experimenting.

The MozVR site (Figure 5-5) features several demos, an integrated user interface for navigating between VR experiences, and a blog with reports on the latest research and projects.

MozVR is still a work in progress, but Josh and the team are dedicated to advancing the state of the art and are keen to collaborate. If you are building something cool with WebVR, they would love to hear from you.

Chapter Summary

In this chapter we delved into the exciting world of WebVR. Today's leading browsers support virtual reality, allowing us to develop VR experiences using open source tools and deliver them to end users without a download or app install. WebVR provides device discovery, fullscreen stereoscopic rendering, and head tracking in a consistent API that allows us to write our apps once and deliver them in all browsers.

Figure 5-5. Sechelt, a virtual reality landscape experience featured on MozVR, Mozilla's showcase site

Developing for WebVR is largely about developing in WebGL. We took a tour of a complete WebVR application written in the popular Three.js library, using WebVR extensions developed by the Mozilla VR research team. We also surveyed several existing WebGL tools and engines that are suitable for creating WebVR apps, including tools we've seen in previous chapters like Unity3D and Unreal, which now have WebGL export capabilities.

WebVR is new, experimental, and not quite ready for prime time. But by tapping into the Web's power of open collaboration, and harnessing the talents of countless committed individuals, it has tremendous potential. WebVR could not only change the playing field for virtual reality development, but actually transform the face of web browsing forever.

CHAPTER 6

VR Everywhere: Google Cardboard for Low-Cost Mobile Virtual Reality

So far we have focused on developing consumer VR for high-end hardware such as the Oculus Rift, HTC Vive, and Samsung Gear VR. These systems can be expensive, costing from several hundred to a few thousand dollars after you factor in peripherals and, potentially, purchasing a new smartphone or computer to power them. Given these prices, the top end of consumer virtual reality is still for enthusiastic early adopters, not the mass market. It would be great if there was a lower-cost VR option for the average consumer, and for developers who aren't ready to make a big financial commitment. Thankfully, we have one such option in Google's *Cardboard VR*.

Google introduced Cardboard VR in 2014 to enable low-cost virtual reality using existing smartphones. The idea was that, by simply dropping a mobile phone into a cardboard box costing about US$2 in parts, anyone can experience VR. Google's original Cardboard VR unit, which debuted at the I/O conference in May 2014, is pictured in Figure 6-1.

By Google's accounting, as of early 2015 more than a million Cardboard headsets had already been distributed—a number that far exceeds the existing installed base of all the high-end systems combined. As we will see later in this chapter, applications written for Cardboard can also be used with several other types of "drop-in" virtual reality stereo viewers, making the potential market for Cardboard applications even larger. Cardboard is also proving to be a popular choice among developers, with hundreds of applications already available for both Android and iOS.

This chapter covers how to build applications for Cardboard VR. There are actually several ways to do this:

- *Use the Cardboard SDK for Android* to create native applications in Java with OpenGL. This is a good option for experienced native developers; however, it only works for Android.
- *Use the Cardboard SDK for Unity* to create native applications with the Unity3D engine. This approach works well for people already conversant with Unity and C# programming, and makes it easy to build for both Android and iOS.
- *Use HTML5, WebGL, and JavaScript* with a mobile browser such as the mobile edition of Chrome or Firefox Mobile to create a web application. If you are most comfortable with web development, and/or you are already creating WebVR desktop applications (see Chapter 5), this might be a good option for you.

Figure 6-1. Google's Cardboard VR viewer

We will go over each of these in some detail. This chapter covers broad territory: three different programming languages and as many development environments. If you can work your way through all of it, you will be approaching VR Jedi status. But if you don't want to, that's OK. Feel free to focus on only the environments you know. If you are most comfortable with native Android, then the first "Developing" section will be the most valuable. If you are a Unity3D developer, or think that Unity is your best bet for covering all the platforms with the least amount of work, then check out the second section. And if you're already a web developer, then the last section will be for you. In this respect, Cardboard VR is kind of like the lottery: many ways to play, more ways to win!

Cardboard Basics

Before we dive into the specifics of developing with each environment, let's get an overview of the world of Cardboard, including the phones and operating systems that can run it, where to buy headsets (or how to build your own), how the technology works in general, and some of the cool applications that have already been built.

Supported Devices and Operating Systems

Cardboard apps run on most Android phones. The original specifications were designed to accommodate phones with screen sizes up to about 5.2 inches, but with the advent of larger phones and phablets, cardboard manufacturers have been making newer headsets that can hold phones with display sizes up to about 6 inches.

Though the scheme was originally designed for use with Android phones, there is actually nothing Android-specific about programming a Cardboard application. Cardboard apps written for iOS run well on newer iPhone models, specifically the iPhone 5 and 6 series.

Cardboard for iOS

As of this writing, the majority of Cardboard VR applications are Android-based, but we can expect to see that change as overall interest in VR increases. I attend and organize quite a few VR meetups in the San Francisco Bay area, and the topic of iOS comes up often. According to many San Francisco–based Cardboard developers, iOS support is one of the most frequent feature requests coming from their users. This may be anecdotal evidence, but it is still telling.

Headset Manufacturers

Cardboard is actually a reference specification. Google doesn't offer it as a product—though it gives plenty of the headsets away at trade shows and marketing events. You get the specifications from Google, and build a headset of your own. The Cardboard specifications can be found at *http://bit.ly/manufacture-cardboard*.

If you don't have the time or inclination to build a Cardboard viewer from scratch, you can also purchase a ready-to-assemble kit from one of several manufacturers, such as DODOcase (*http://www.dodocase.com/*), I Am Cardboard (*http://www.imcardboard.com/*), Knox Labs (*http://www.knoxlabs.com/*), and Unofficial Cardboard (*https://www.unofficialcardboard.com/*). In addition to selling headset kits, each of these manufacturers also provides a mobile app, downloadable from the Google Play Store and/or the iTunes Store, that provides a handy list of Cardboard-ready VR applications.

Other drop-in virtual reality headsets

As it turns out, Cardboard isn't the only mobile phone–based virtual reality viewing system; in fact, it wasn't even the first. There are several other "drop-in" viewers on the market. These headsets are made from a variety of materials, such as hard plastic and foam rubber, and come in different form factors with different lens shapes, distortion methods, and fields of view. They tend to cost more than the Cardboard, typically being priced at around US$100. Here are a few of the notable products:

- The *Durovis Dive* (*http://www.durovis.com/*), arguably the first smartphone VR headset, came out well before Google's Cardboard.
- *MergeVR* (*http://mergevr.com/*) makes the Merge Goggles, a durable foam rubber headset that also comes with Bluetooth input devices to enhance the experience. The MergeVR headset is depicted in Figure 6-2.
- The *Wearality Sky* (*http://wearality.com/*), a newer entry to the market, features a comfortable lightweight plastic frame and a wide field of view. Wearality glasses can view standard Cardboard content adequately, but work even better when applications have been designed to take advantage of the wider field of view.

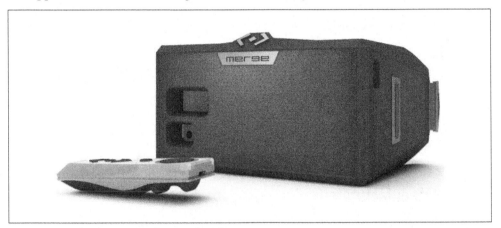

Figure 6-2. The MergeVR drop-in headset

Each of these headsets comes with its own Android and/or Unity SDKs that fully exploit the device's various features. This could be a recipe for chaos, requiring developers to create custom builds for each device—but thankfully, the rise in popularity of the Cardboard specification has forced most of the manufacturers to support Cardboard in a compatibility mode. To cut a long story short, most of the techniques described in this chapter should work with the other drop-in headsets right out of the box, and you can be confident that your Cardboard app will run fairly well on them.

Cardboard Applications

Go to the Google Play Store (*https://play.google.com/store*) and type "Cardboard VR" into the search box. You will find hundreds of applications, including games, 360-degree video and photo viewers, educational simulations, and at least two ports of Oculus's famous Tuscany demo (see Chapter 1). Given the low cost of manufacturing, Cardboard seems like a natural fit for live events and advertising campaigns: it has already powered VR experiences with big-name entertainers like Sir Paul McCartney and Jack White, and brands such as Volvo. Not surprisingly, games make up the lion's share of entries in the Play Store; one example is Sharks VR (*http://bit.ly/sharksvr*), the undersea adventure game depicted in Figure 6-3.

Figure 6-3. Sharks VR, an undersea VR adventure game

The Cardboard demo application allows you to launch applications by tapping one of the icons, or you can use the novel virtual reality interface to start its featured applications from within the app itself. The VR launcher mode is shown in Figure 6-5.

The Play Store also features several "launcher" apps, which present a curated list of VR applications that makes it easier for users to find the best experiences. Most of the headset makers provide launcher apps to go with their Cardboard device; Google's demo application, named simply Cardboard (*http://bit.ly/cardboard-demo*), is pictured in Figure 6-4.

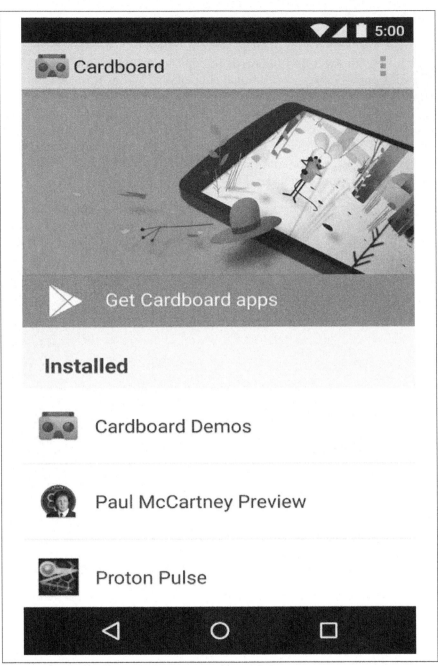

Figure 6-4. Google's Cardboard demo application

Many of the launcher apps from other Cardboard VR headset makers contain similar VR exploration modes, such as the DODOcase VR App Store (*http://bit.ly/dodocase-vr*) application.

Figure 6-5. Google's Cardboard demo application in VR launcher mode

Input Devices for Cardboard

Input for Cardboard VR can be challenging. The phone is fully contained inside a box, so the user doesn't have access to the most commonly used mobile input mechanism: the touch screen. Different makers of Cardboard and other drop-in headsets have devised different solutions to this problem.

Google's input device is shown in the image of the Cardboard headset depicted in Figure 6-1. There is a metal ring on the upper left of the headset, on which you pull downward when you want to select something in the VR scene. The ring is actually a magnet, and there is a second magnet on the inside of the box. By pulling down on the magnet, the user is perturbing a magnetic field, and this perturbation is detected by the magnetometer on the phone. This is a brilliant solution! But while the magnet switch works very well, it doesn't work with all phones, because it is highly dependent on the position of the magnet on the phone. The magnet switch also only works with Android native code; it can't be used with iOS or in mobile browsers, because HTML5 browsers do not support an API for detecting changes to the phone's magnetic sensor.

DODOcase, another popular Cardboard manufacturer, wasn't satisfied with the lack of device coverage provided by the magnet switch, so its developers devised a completely different mechanism (Figure 6-6). A wooden stick protrudes from the upper-right side of the headset. Pressing downward on the stick causes a piece of capacitive plastic inside the headset to bend and touch the phone's touch screen, essentially mimicking a finger tap. This is also a brilliant solution, and more universal than the magnet switch: it works with many more Android phones, as well as iPhones and mobile browsers on both platforms.

Figure 6-6. The DODOcase Cardboard viewer with universal input switch

While the DODOcase input switch is a step in the right direction, it is still experimental and made of inexpensive materials. (No, you're not imagining things; that is indeed a Popsicle stick protruding from the box!) It was devised for early developers and experimenters to play with. If it ever becomes widely adopted, the company can make it out of something more durable.

Other Cardboard makers are experimenting with more sophisticated input devices, such as Bluetooth-connected game controllers. The Sharks VR app shown in Figure 6-3, for example, uses a game controller. Also, some headset companies are working on new types of Bluetooth controllers specifically designed for VR; note the plastic controller shown in the foreground of the MergeVR screenshot in Figure 6-2. But each of these kinds of controllers requires custom programming, and as of this writing, there is no standardized, widely adopted input mechanism for mobile VR.

This lack of a standardized input device has led to many apps being designed to use *gaze tracking*—that is, detecting where the user is looking—combined with either a single tap or a timer countdown indicated by an animated cursor. We will see examples of both later in the chapter.

Cardboard Stereo Rendering and Head Tracking

The Cardboard VR approach to stereo rendering is simpler than the Oculus Rift's: it is a 90-degree horizontal field of view without the barrel distortion. This allows applications to do simple side-by-side rendering in two viewports, one for each eye. Figure 6-7 shows an example of a 3D scene rendered side by side for Cardboard, from the app *Stadiums for Cardboard VR*.

Figure 6-7. Side-by-side rendering from Stadiums for Cardboard VR (http://bit.ly/ stadiums-cardboard)

Head tracking in Cardboard VR is also a bit simpler than with the Rift. It uses the existing operating system orientation events generated by the phone's compass and accelerometer, collectively known as the *inertial measurement unit* (IMU). Note that today's phone operating systems typically deliver IMU changes at less than 60 frames per second. This is slower than the 75–120 FPS targets cited by Oculus and other high-end HMD makers; however, because of the smaller field of view, most users find the slower tracking acceptable, at least for short experiences.

The details of programming the stereo rendering and head tracking differ greatly between native Android, Unity3D-based applications, and HTML5 web code. And yet the principles are the same for all of them: render the scene twice—once for each eye with a natural stereo separation—and update the camera based on the IMU's orientation.

So Is Cardboard VR Good Enough VR?

Because of the 60 FPS head tracking, the narrower field of view, and, for older phones, the lower display resolution (compared to the Samsung Galaxy Note 4's sexy 1280x1440 pixels per eye), many VR insiders consider Cardboard VR an inferior experience. Clearly, that is a subjective assessment. Proponents of Cardboard argue that the generally lower-end experiences are acceptable for shorter periods of use—i.e., "bite-size" VR that makes the medium more affordable and thus accessible to more people.

Also, it is worth keeping in mind that the Cardboard team at Google aren't sitting still. They know the current limitations better than anybody, and have alluded to making changes in future versions of Android to address both the field of view and tracking speed limitations. So it's possible that a future version of Cardboard will get closer to parity with higher-end VR platforms.

Developing with the Cardboard SDK for Android

In this section we will explore Java-based development of native Android VR applications. If you are not interested in using Java and OpenGL to create Cardboard applications for Android, or need to run an app that will also run on iOS, feel free to skip this section and move on to the sections on Unity3D and HTML5.

Google's Java-based SDK, known as the *Cardboard SDK for Android*, comes with a ready-to-build sample application and a detailed tutorial. There is no reason to duplicate all of that information here, and to do so would be beyond the scope of this book. But we will take a look at the highlights so that we can get a feel for the tools, technical concepts, and development process. The SDK example is a Treasure Hunt game, depicted in Figure 6-8.

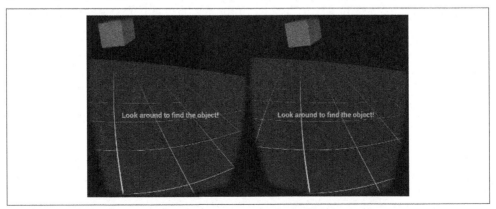

Figure 6-8. Treasure Hunt sample included with the Cardboard SDK for Android

The object of the game is simple: look for cubes floating in space. When you gaze over one, it highlights; pull down on the magnet to select it. The cube then disappears, and you score a point and are prompted to look around for another one. Then you do it again. It's not the most satisfying gameplay, but it does illustrate core Cardboard development concepts:

- Creating a stereo view rendered in OpenGL
- Using gaze tracking to select objects
- Using the magnet switch for input

Setting Up the Environment

Google has done an excellent job of documenting the steps for creating your first native Cardboard application. To get going, visit the main Android SDK page (*http://bit.ly/cardboard-sdk*), where you will find links and instructions for downloading the tools and samples, as well as complete tutorials.

As of this writing, native Cardboard development is best done using *Android Studio*, a new integrated development environment (IDE) dubbed "the official Android IDE." Android Studio is supplanting Eclipse as the main visual development tool for Android. (You may recall that Eclipse is the development tool currently being used to create Gear VR applications, as described in Chapter 4.) Figure 6-9 shows a screenshot of Android Studio.

While Android Studio is much improved over Eclipse, it has similar issues in that setup and configuration can be frustratingly hard. Make sure to carefully follow the instructions at the official site (*http://bit.ly/android-studio-dev*) and refer to various online documentation sources on how to set up emulators for testing and how to build for specific phone devices.

Walking Through the Code

The "Getting Started" (*http://bit.ly/cardboard-started*) section of the Android SDK documentation has a complete walkthrough of the Treasure Hunt sample app. Let's take a look at some of the more interesting parts.

Creating and rendering a stereo view

The first thing we need to do is create a main application view: in this case, a full-screen Android view that we will use to render the 3D scene in stereo. We do this by creating a new Android *activity* that represents the application. The source code for this activity, implemented in the Java class MainActivity, resides in the file *MainActivity.java*. Let's look at the first line of the class definition:

```
/**
 * A Cardboard sample application.
 */
public class MainActivity extends CardboardActivity
    implements CardboardView.StereoRenderer {

    ... // class code for MainActivity here

}
```

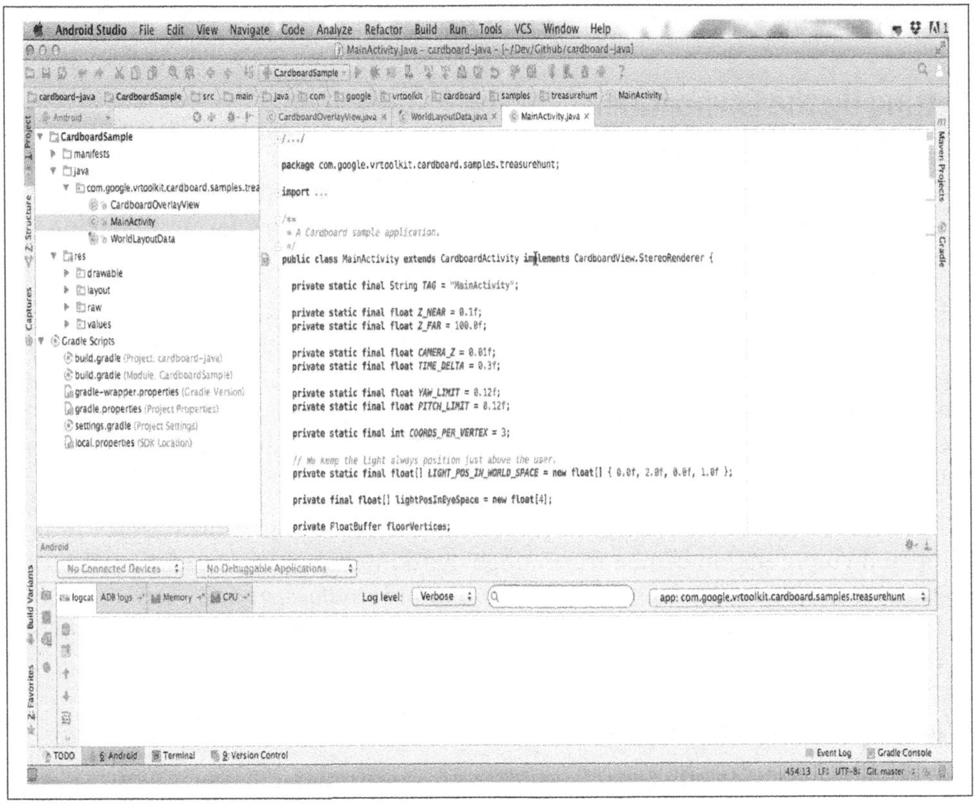

Figure 6-9. Android Studio, version 1.2

The SDK supplies a CardboardActivity class that all Cardboard applications can extend. CardboardActivity provides easy integration with Cardboard devices, by exposing events to interact with Cardboard headsets and handling many of the details commonly required when creating an activity for VR rendering. You don't have to implement this interface in your code, but by doing so you will save yourself a lot of work. In addition to extending CardboardActivity, your main application class should implement the interface CardboardView.StereoRenderer along with a couple of rendering methods specific to your application, as we will see.

The first method your class should implement is onNewFrame(), which is called by the SDK each time the application is ready to draw the view—that is, for each *frame* (also known as a tick, time slice, or update cycle). Your application should use this method to perform per-frame updates that are not specific to either eye, such as updating objects in the scene and tracking the current head position. The method definition follows:

```
/**
 * Prepares OpenGL ES before we draw a frame.
 *
 * @param headTransform The head transformation in the new frame.
 */
@Override
public void onNewFrame(HeadTransform headTransform) {
    // Build the Model part of the ModelView matrix.
    Matrix.rotateM(modelCube, 0, TIME_DELTA, 0.5f, 0.5f,
    f1.0f);

    // Build the camera matrix and apply it to the ModelView.
    Matrix.setLookAtM(camera, 0, 0.0f, 0.0f, CAMERA_Z,
        0.0f, 0.0f, 0.0f, 0.0f, 1.0f, 0.0f);

    headTransform.getHeadView(headView, 0);

    checkGLError("onReadyToDraw");
}
```

Our version of this method does two things: 1) it rotates the cube by updating values in the modelCube and camera matrices associated with it; and 2) it uses the headTransform helper class to track the phone's orientation, saving the values into the class member headView. headView will be used later to do gaze tracking.

Now that we have taken care of per-frame updates, it's time to draw. Because we are doing stereo rendering for Cardboard, we actually draw the scene twice, once from each eye. This is done in the method onDrawEye():

```
public void onDrawEye(Eye eye) {
    GLES20.glClear(GLES20.GL_COLOR_BUFFER_BIT | GLES20.GL_DEPTH_BUFFER_BIT);

    checkGLError("colorParam");

    // Apply the eye transformation to the camera.
    Matrix.multiplyMM(view, 0, eye.getEyeView(), 0, camera, 0);

    // Set the position of the light.
    Matrix.multiplyMV(lightPosInEyeSpace, 0, view, 0, LIGHT_POS_IN_WORLD_SPACE, 0);

    // Build the ModelView and ModelViewProjection matrices
    // for calculating cube position and light.
    float[] perspective = eye.getPerspective(Z_NEAR, Z_FAR);
    Matrix.multiplyMM(modelView, 0, view, 0, modelCube, 0);
```

```
    Matrix.multiplyMM(modelViewProjection, 0, perspective, 0, modelView, 0);
    drawCube();

    // Set modelView for the floor, so we draw the floor in the correct location.
    Matrix.multiplyMM(modelView, 0, view, 0, modelFloor, 0);
    Matrix.multiplyMM(modelViewProjection, 0, perspective, 0,
        modelView, 0);
    drawFloor();
}
```

onDrawEye() is called by the SDK once for each eye. It takes as an argument an Eye object, which contains information on the world space position and perspective projection for each eye. Let's walk through what this method does, step by step:

1. Save the eye information into the matrix view, for use in subsequent matrix calculations.
2. Calculate the scene light's position in view space. This will be used to shade the cube and floor.
3. Calculate the cube's position in view space using the current values of the model View and the modelCube matrix (calculated previously in the method onNew Frame()).
4. Draw the cube by calling the helper method drawCube(). That method will draw the cube either normally or highlighted in yellow, depending on whether the user is looking at it. We will cover that in the next section when we discuss gaze tracking.
5. Calculate the floor's position in view space using the current values of the model View and the modelFloor matrix.
6. Draw the floor by calling the helper method drawFloor().

The Smartphone as Reality Engine

Now that we have walked through our rendering code, it's worth taking a step back and reflecting on how far computers have come in a short time. In this sample app—admittedly a simple one—onDrawEye() does all this work, calculating matrices, setting up vertex and color buffers, drawing to the OpenGL hardware pipeline...

every frame...

once for each eye...

60 times per second...

on a phone.

Think about that for a minute.

Selecting objects using gaze tracking

As noted, `drawCube()` renders the cube either normally or if the user is looking at it, highlighted in yellow. This technique is known as *gaze tracking*. Let's see how we do it. The details are implemented in the helper method `isLookingAtObject()`:

```
/**
 * Check if user is looking at object by calculating where the object is in
 * eye-space.
 *
 * @return true if the user is looking at the object.
 */
private boolean isLookingAtObject() {
  float[] initVec = { 0, 0, 0, 1.0f };
  float[] objPositionVec = new float[4];

  // Convert object space to camera space. Use the headView from onNewFrame.
  Matrix.multiplyMM(modelView, 0, headView, 0, modelCube, 0);
  Matrix.multiplyMV(objPositionVec, 0, modelView, 0, initVec, 0);

  float pitch = (float) Math.atan2(objPositionVec[1], -objPositionVec[2]);
  float yaw = (float) Math.atan2(objPositionVec[0], -objPositionVec[2]);

  return Math.abs(pitch) < PITCH_LIMIT && Math.abs(yaw) < YAW_LIMIT;
}
```

We determine whether the user is looking at the object by figuring out the angle between the eye view vector (i.e., the direction the user is looking in) and the location of the center of the object. If the angle is smaller than a certain rotation about the *x*- and *y*-axes (also known as *pitch* and *yaw*), then the user is looking at the object. The math in here might seem a bit counterintuitive, but it is a straightforward and fast way to calculate the intersection, in contrast to intersecting a pick ray with the object—and it is accurate enough for this simple demo. Here's how it works:

1. Calculate the cube's position relative to the camera space, by multiplying the cube's model and view matrices and then multiplying that result by an origin vector (`initVec`).
2. Calculate the rotation between the cube's origin in camera space and the origin of the camera itself in camera space, which is, by definition, at the actual origin (`0, 0, 0`).
3. Use trigonometry (the `Math.atan2()` function) to find the rotation between the cube's position and the camera's position, in both the *x* and *y* dimensions.
4. If the *x* and *y* rotations are within the defined limits `PITCH_LIMIT` and `YAW_LIMIT`, return `true`; otherwise, return `false`.

Detecting input from the magnet switch

Now we just need to figure out when the user presses the magnet switch and "finds the treasure"—i.e., if the user is looking at the cube when the switch is pressed. To do this, we can override `CardboardActivity.onCardboardTrigger()` in our application's activity. This method is called by the SDK when the switch is pressed. When this happens in our app we update the score, change the prompt in the overlay, and hide the cube. (Actually, we don't hide the cube; we move it to another random position out of the user's current view, so that we are ready for the next round.) As a flourish, we also vibrate the phone to provide additional user feedback:

```
/**
 * Called when the Cardboard trigger is pulled.
 */
@Override
public void onCardboardTrigger() {
  Log.i(TAG, "onCardboardTrigger");

    if (isLookingAtObject()) {
    score++;
    overlayView.show3DToast(
        "Found it! Look around for another one.\nScore = " + score);
    hideObject();
    } else {
    overlayView.show3DToast("Look around to find the object!");
  }

    // Always give user feedback.
    vibrator.vibrate(50);
}
```

Developing with the Cardboard SDK for Unity

Google's Cardboard tools come with support for creating applications in the popular Unity3D game engine. The main page of the Cardboard SDK for Unity can be found at *http://bit.ly/csdk-unity*. It contains a Unity3D version of the Treasure Hunt example (see the previous section), and a rich developer guide and programming reference. Let's walk through building Treasure Hunt for Unity.

Setting Up the SDK

To get set up, follow the instructions on the download page (*http://bit.ly/csdk-unity-samples*). We can summarize the steps here:

1. First, make sure you have a recent version of Unity3D. To build the examples in the book, I used Unity 5 Pro. You can always find the latest version at *http://bit.ly/unity-dl*. If you're not familiar with Unity, or are feeling a bit rusty, refer to the extensive information in Chapter 3.

2. Next, get the Cardboard SDK for Unity. This is available as a direct download, or in source code form at Google's GitHub repository (*http://bit.ly/cardboard-github*).
3. If you don't already have it, install the Android SDK (*http://bit.ly/android-sdk-dl*). This is the SDK for general Android development, not just VR. The Unity packages require it. If you do have the Android SDK, make sure to update it.

Now, you are ready to start using the Cardboard SDK for Unity. The SDK is a Unity package that you import into your project. So, start by creating an empty Unity project. Call it *UnityCardboardTest*, so that we're all on the same page. Now that the project has been created, we will import the SDK into it and build the Treasure Hunt sample.

Figure 6-10 shows a screenshot of the package importing process.

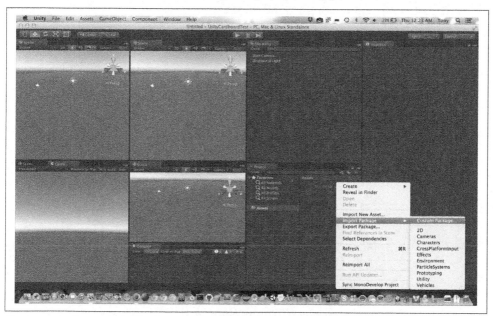

Figure 6-10. Importing the Cardboard SDK package into a Unity project

To import the Cardboard SDK package into the new project, follow these steps:

1. Find the Assets pane of the Project tab in the Unity IDE. Choose Assets → Import Package → Custom Package.
2. You should see a file dialog box. Use it to navigate to the location of the downloaded Unity SDK.
3. Select the file *CardboardSDKForUnity.unitypackage*. If you downloaded the file by cloning the GitHub repo, you will find this file in the root directory.

4. Once you have clicked Open, Unity will scan the file and present you with a list of package contents to import. For now, let's just bring them all into the project: make sure that all of the objects in the list are checked, and click the Import button. You will now see assets present in the Assets pane, where there were none before.

You're good to go! You can now build Cardboard VR applications using Unity.

Building Treasure Hunt for Unity

Once you have imported the Cardboard SDK into your project, it's really easy to build the Treasure Hunt demo. The demo comes packaged with the SDK, so it is already in your project, and in just a few steps you can have it running on your phone. The demo is pictured in Figure 6-11. Note that the Unity version has a nice touch: a dynamic particle system floating around the cube.

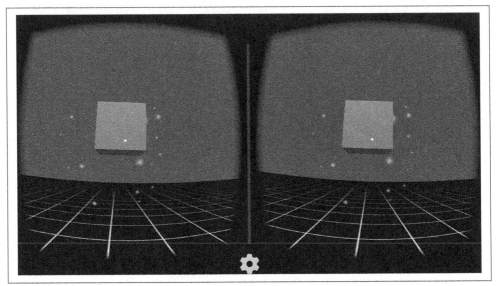

Figure 6-11. The Unity3D version of Treasure Hunt

To add the assets for Treasure Hunt to the new project, select the folder *Assets/Cardboard/DemoScene*. In the detail pane you will see an icon for a Unity scene named *DemoScene*; double-click that icon. You should now see the scene in the main editor view. You can hit the Play button at the top of the Unity window to get a preview on your computer.

To build the app for your phone, you need to change a couple of settings. First, open the Build Settings dialog by selecting File → Build Settings from the main menu. You will see a dialog that resembles the screenshot in Figure 6-12.

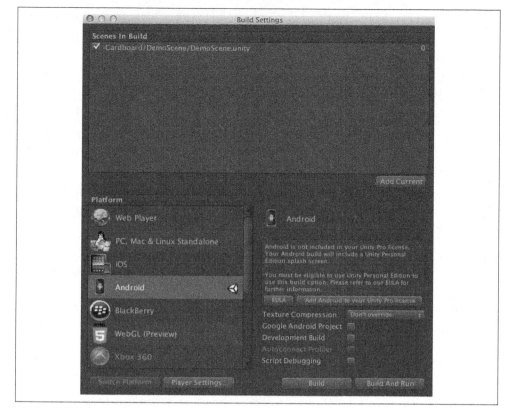

Figure 6-12. Build settings for the Treasure Hunt Android app

Now perform the following steps:

1. Select Android in the list of platforms and then click the Switch Platform button.
2. Add the demo scene to your build. The Scenes In Build list at the top will be empty to start; you need to add the current scene. You should already be viewing it in the editor view; clicking the Add Current button will add it to the list, and you will see a checked item named *Cardboard/DemoScene/DemoScene.unity*.
3. Click the Player Settings button on the bottom left. This will open the Inspector, displaying the Player Settings panel. (You should see it on the far right of the Unity interface.) Find the setting named Bundle Identifier, and change its value to a reasonable Android package name. Make sure to change it from the default value, or Unity will complain during the build step. I used the value *vr.cardboard.UnityCardboardTest*.
4. Finally, go back to the Build Settings dialog and click the Build And Run button. You will be prompted for a filename under which to save the *.apk* (Android pack-

age) file. I chose the name *UnityCardboardTest.apk*. That's the name that will show up on the phone in your list of apps. Hit Save to save the *.apk*.

The app should now launch. Pop it into your Cardboard viewer and play!

A Walkthrough of the Unity Code

With the Cardboard SDK in place, it's surprisingly easy to build a working Cardboard application using Unity. Most of the work takes place in the Unity editor: construct the 3D scene using the visual editor, drop in the prefabs from the Cardboard SDK, and implement a little bit of logic.

For the Treasure Hunt demo, we simply need to detect the gaze/tap combination and move the highlighted cube to a new location. Let's see how this is put together. The first stop is the Unity editor:

- In the editor, select the cube. You can do this by either clicking directly on the cube in one of the Scene views or clicking on the name of the object (*Cube*) in the Hierarchy pane.
- Now, go to the Inspector pane. You should see several properties, grouped into subpanes. Scroll to the bottom and you will see three Event Trigger properties: one each for Pointer Enter and Exit, and one for Pointer Click (see the blue out-lined areas in Figure 6-13).

The Cardboard SDK comes with a module called `GazeInputModule`, which manages when the camera is looking at objects. When the user's gaze shifts to a new object, this module converts that into a standard Unity pointer event, treating it as if the mouse pointer had rolled over the object on a desktop monitor. `GazeInputModule` also handles magnet switch and touch screen events such that, if those input actions take place, they are delivered to the currently gazed-at object and treated as though they were mouse clicks. By supplying the values `Teleport.SetGazedAt` and `Teleport.TeleportRandomly` in the property sheet, we are telling the Unity runtime to call those named methods in response to the gaze events. With this simple wiring in place, all that's left to do is actually handle the actions in a script.

Note the property value annotated with the red arrow in Figure 6-13. This is the name of the script that implements the event triggers: in our case, a script class named `Teleport`. Double-click on this value and MonoDevelop, Unity's code editor for C# programmers, will open the file *Teleport.cs* from the project sources. The entirety of the class implementation is in the following code listing:

```
// Copyright 2014 Google Inc. All rights reserved.
...

using UnityEngine;
using System.Collections;
```

```
[RequireComponent(typeof(Collider))]
public class Teleport : MonoBehaviour {
  private Vector3 startingPosition;

  void Start() {
    startingPosition = transform.localPosition;
    SetGazedAt(false);
  }

  public void SetGazedAt(bool gazedAt) {
    GetComponent<Renderer>().material.color = gazedAt ? Color.green : Color.red;
  }

  public void Reset() {
    transform.localPosition = startingPosition;
  }

  public void TeleportRandomly() {
    Vector3 direction = Random.onUnitSphere;
    direction.y = Mathf.Clamp(direction.y, 0.5f, 1f);
    float distance = 2 * Random.value + 1.5f;
    transform.localPosition = direction * distance;
  }
}
```

Teleport is defined as a subclass of MonoBehaviour, which is the base class for all scripts. The script only does two important things:

1. The method SetGazedAt() highlights the cube in green if it is being gazed at; otherwise, it sets the color to red. Visual objects in Unity contain a Renderer component; we simply set the color of its material to either green or red.
2. The method TeleportRandomly() uses the Unity built-in class Random to generate a random direction vector on a unit sphere and move the cube a random distance along that vector.

And that's actually it. Unity is such a powerful, professional 3D authoring system that putting together applications like this is almost trivial—once you master the intricacies of the interface. Combining the Cardboard SDK with Unity, we were able to put together a basic Cardboard demo in no time at all.

Developing Cardboard Applications Using HTML5 and a Mobile Browser

If you worked through the Unity Cardboard project in the previous section, you saw how simple putting together an app can be using pro tools. Well, now we are going to survey the Wild West of developing Cardboard applications using a mobile browser. There are few tools to speak of; we'll have to cobble our code together from open source libraries. But on the plus side, at the end we will have a no-download Cardboard VR application that we can launch just by opening a link in a web browser!

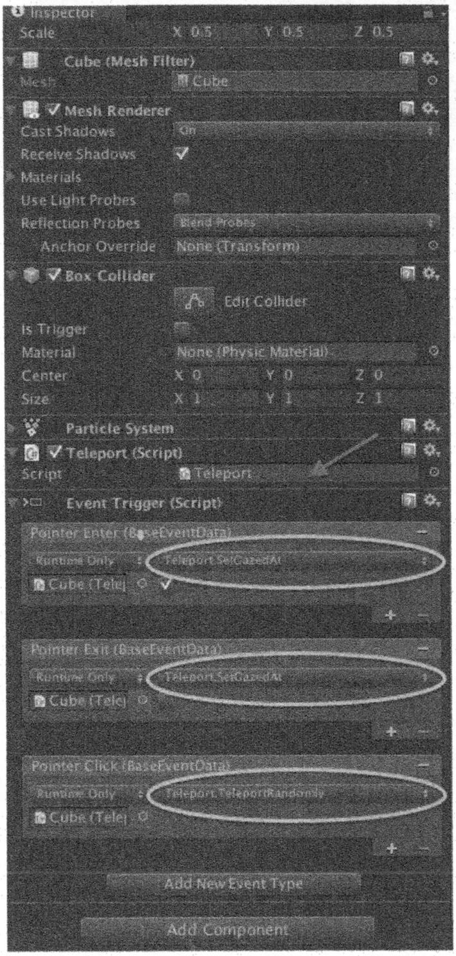

Figure 6-13. Setting up scripting and event triggers for the cube's Teleport script

Developing Cardboard web applications is a little different from using the WebVR APIs we looked at in Chapter 5; however, there are also many similarities. We code in HTML5 and JavaScript and render using WebGL, typically with a library like Three.js. Figure 6-14 shows a Cardboard version of the simple WebVR example we coded in the previous chapter.

You can run this app live by visiting the URL *http://bit.ly/cardboard-vr-cube* in your mobile browser. Once the page opens, you will see a rotating cube with the WebVR logo, rendered in Cardboard stereo. Tap the Start VR Mode button to put the page into fullscreen mode. Then pop the phone into your Cardboard viewer, and you can look around the scene. You should see the cube move.

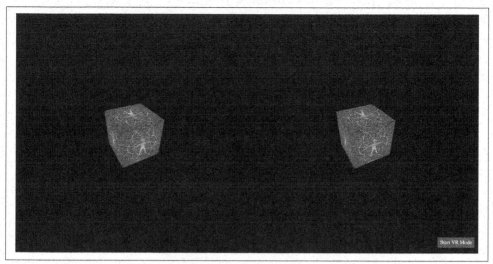

Figure 6-14. WebVR sample application for Cardboard

Setting Up the WebVR Project

To look through the code for this example, please clone the GitHub repository (*https://github.com/tparisi/WebVR*).

If you also want to preview this file and/or make changes to it, you will need to run it from a local web server. Chapter 5 contains instructions for how to set one up simply, if you're not sure how to do that.

The JavaScript Cardboard Code

Let's walk through the JavaScript code for this example. The source code is in the file */examples/cube-cardboard.html*. The application is written using the Three.js library for WebGL development. (If you're not familiar with Three.js, refer to the information on it in Chapter 5.)

First, we have the main application, defined in a jQuery `ready()` callback function that is called when the page is loaded and ready:

```
$(document).ready(
        function() {

                // Set up Three.js
                initThreeJS();

                // Set up VR rendering
```

```
            initVREffect();

            // Create the scene content
            initScene();

            // Set up VR camera controls
            initVRControls();

            // Run the run loop
            run();
        }
    );
```

The `ready()` callback function calls several helper functions, also defined in this file. Let's go through each one. First, we set up stereo rendering and fullscreen mode:

```
function initVREffect() {
    // Set up Cardboard renderer
    effect = new THREE.StereoEffect(renderer);
    effect.setSize(window.innerWidth, window.innerHeight);

    // StereoEffect's default separation is in cm, we're in M
    // Actual cardboard eye separation is 2.5 in
    // Finally, separation is per-eye, so divide by 2
    effect.separation = 2.5 * 0.0254 / 2;

    // Set up fullscreen mode handling
    var fullScreenButton = document.querySelector( '.button' );
    fullScreenButton.onclick = function() {
        if ( container.mozRequestFullScreen ) {
            container.mozRequestFullScreen();
        } else {
            container.webkitRequestFullscreen();
        }
    };
}
```

In `initVREffect()`, we set up Cardboard VR stereo rendering using the `THREE.StereoEffect` class. This class was designed to render a scene in WebGL twice, side by side, using Cardboard's recommended camera values with a 90-degree field of view and typical interpupillary offsets for the two cameras. In addition to setting up the renderer, we also have the code to handle going into fullscreen mode when the button is pressed. This uses standard web browser methods for entering fullscreen mode, which, historically, use browser-specific prefixes depending on whether we are using Firefox Mobile (`mozRequestFullScreen()`) or a WebKit-based browser such as mobile Chrome or Safari (`webkitRequestFullScreen()`).

Next, we initialize the scene, using various Three.js objects to create a scene with a camera and a textured cube:

```
function initScene() {
    // Create a new Three.js scene
    scene = new THREE.Scene();

    // Add  a camera so we can view the scene
    camera = new THREE.PerspectiveCamera( 90,
                window.innerWidth / window.innerHeight, 1, 4000 );
    scene.add(camera);

    // Create a texture-mapped cube and add it to the scene
    // First, create the texture map
    var mapUrl = "../images/webvr-logo-512.jpeg";
    var map = THREE.ImageUtils.loadTexture(mapUrl);

    // Now, create a Basic material; pass in the map
    var material = new THREE.MeshBasicMaterial({ map: map });

    // Create the cube geometry
    var geometry = new THREE.BoxGeometry(2, 2, 2);

    // And put the geometry and material together into a mesh
    cube = new THREE.Mesh(geometry, material);

    // Move the mesh back from the camera and tilt it toward the viewer
    cube.position.z = -6;
    cube.rotation.x = Math.PI / 5;
    cube.rotation.y = Math.PI / 5;

    // Finally, add the mesh to our scene
    scene.add( cube );

}
```

Now it's time to set up the camera controller. This object updates the camera's orientation to match the phone's orientation, based on IMU input. HTML5 mobile browsers come with a *device orientation API* that delivers IMU changes to the application in the form of `orientationchange` DOM events; `THREE.DeviceOrientationControls` handles those events and automatically updates the camera we passed in to its constructor whenever it detects a change:

```
function initVRControls() {
    // Set up VR camera controls
    controls = new THREE.DeviceOrientationControls(camera);
}
```

Our application is fully set up; now we need to run it. We do this by creating a run loop, a function that drives continuous animation and rendering of 3D scenes. The run loop is driven by a built-in browser function, `requestAnimationFrame()`, which calls our application every time the browser is ready to re-render the page. The following listing shows the run loop for this example:

```
var duration = 10000; // ms
function animate(deltat) {
    var fract = deltat / duration;
    var angle = Math.PI * 2 * fract;
    cube.rotation.y += angle;
}

var lastTime = 0;
function run(time) {
    requestAnimationFrame(run);
    var dt = time - lastTime;
    lastTime = time;
    // Render the scene
    effect.render( scene, camera );

    // Update the VR camera controls
    controls.update();

    // Spin the cube for next frame
    animate(dt);
}
```

Chapter 5 contains a lengthy walkthrough of the run loop for the Oculus Rift version of this same example, so we won't go into all the details here; the broad strokes are that, each time through the run loop, the application renders the scene, updates the camera based on device orientation, and animates the cube.

Chapter Summary

This chapter explored the basics of developing for Cardboard VR, an affordable way to experience virtual reality using just about any smartphone and an inexpensive drop-in headset. Cardboard uses simple stereo rendering and the phone's built-in accelerometer to deliver modest but fun VR at a fraction of the cost of the high-end headsets on the market today.

Cardboard development can take on many forms. We can program in Java using Android Studio and Google's native Android SDK; we can build Unity3D applications in C# using the Unity editor and an SDK developed by Google; or we can create no-download, mobile browser–based Cardboard VR apps using JavaScript and HTML5. Which environment is right for you depends on a combination of your needs and preferences; regardless, coding is straightforward in all of them.

In this chapter we also took a first look at an essential technique for designing virtual reality user interfaces: gaze tracking. By detecting where the user is looking, we can highlight or select objects, and trigger behaviors based on touch input. We will revisit gaze tracking in the next chapter, when we build our first full VR application.

Cardboard VR may be low-end, but it's fun. While it doesn't provide the transcendent, full immersion of high-end VR, Cardboard is a low-cost, low-commitment way to create and experience VR today.

CHAPTER 7

Your First VR Application

In previous chapters, we learned the basic techniques of virtual reality development. We also surveyed various VR platforms coming to market, as well as the popular tools used to create VR. In this final chapter, we are going to put this all together and create an end-to-end application.

Given the time and space constraints of a book, we can't really build a production-quality app; but we can go through, in fine detail, the steps required to create a meaningful VR experience with simple user interaction. For the exercise, we will focus on an app that is immediately understandable by everyone: a panoramic photo viewer for smartphones, using Google Cardboard VR.

Figure 7-1 shows a screenshot from my Nexus 5: a 360-degree panoramic photo of Yosemite National Park, rendered side by side for Cardboard. At the bottom of the screen are four semitransparent image thumbnails. Gazing over any thumbnail makes it turn opaque (i.e., "selects" it); touching the magnet switch on the side of the Cardboard viewer will change the panorama to the selected image. This is what we are going to build.

Recall that, when developing for Cardboard, we have several choices of tools and languages. We can use Unity3D, currently the most popular VR development environment; we can go with Java-based native Android development, via the Android Studio IDE; or we can write web code for mobile browsers, using a JavaScript-based VR framework such as Three.js. In the end, I decided to go with Unity3D for this final chapter. Unity is not only popular, it's good: it has many useful graphical, drag-and-drop capabilities that allow us to focus on designing the application, rather than on the plumbing. That said, the user interface is also a bit quirky to work with, so if you're not well versed in Unity make sure to follow the instructions carefully.

Figure 7-1. A simple 360-degree photo viewer for Android

In developing a simple 360 photo viewer for Cardboard, we will review many of the topics we have covered so far in the book, including:

- Creating a 3D scene
- Using the Unity3D engine and editor to develop VR
- Using the Cardboard SDK to render the scene in stereo, and track motions of the head using the phone's accelerometer
- Creating a gaze-and-tap interface of the style being used in many VR applications
- Building an app for Android

The photo viewer we are going to build makes heavy use of Google's Cardboard SDK for Unity, described in Chapter 6. Feel free to review that chapter if you feel like you need a refresher.

About 360-Degree Panoramas

360-degree panoramic photos are becoming more commonplace. There are several iOS applications available that allow consumers to take 360 panoramas by simply tapping the screen and moving the phone around in all directions; the application takes care of stitching the image into a seamless panorama, with generally good results. Many Android phones, such as the Samsung Note 4 and the Google Nexus 5, come with panoramic photo applications already bundled.

A 360 panorama is simply a specially laid out image stored in a standard image format such as PNG or JPEG. The layout is known as an *equirectangular projection*, derived from a traditional map projection that goes back almost two thousand years. The image file for the panorama depicted in Figure 7-1, when viewed in a rectangular viewport instead of on a sphere, is shown in Figure 7-2.

Figure 7-2. A 360-degree panoramic with equirectangular projection

If you're like me, you probably don't care how equirectangular projection actually works; you're just happy that it does. But if you're map-curious, the Wikipedia entry (*http://bit.ly/equirectangular-proj*) contains extensive information.

Setting Up the Project

First, we are going to set up the basic Unity project, creating the geometry objects and importing the assets required to make a 3D scene with a panoramic background from photos. At the moment, it doesn't need to run on Android or with Cardboard. In fact, we'll just build and preview it on the desktop, to make sure we have a correctly set up 3D scene.

Getting the Software, Hardware, and Sample Code

If you want to re-create the project step by step, you will need to get the following:

1. Unity3D version 5.1 or higher. To download and install Unity on your computer, go to *http://unity3d.com/get-unity* and follow the instructions.
2. The Cardboard SDK for Unity. The main page can be found at *http://bit.ly/csdk-unity*.
3. A Cardboard viewer with a side-mounted magnet switch. If you need to purchase one, Chapter 6 and Appendix A both contain lists of Google-approved Cardboard vendors.

4. An Android smartphone capable of running Cardboard VR well. I used my Nexus 5 phone to build and test the application.

5. The code for the application, which can be found on GitHub (*https://github.com/ tparisi/LearningVirtualReality*). The folder *Unity Code* contains the assets you will drop into various places in the Unity project, if you decided to follow along with the examples step by step. The folder *360Viewer* contains a completed Unity project, which you can feel free to borrow from liberally.

Creating the Unity Scene and Project

Create a new Unity project. Name it *360Viewer*. Unity will create a default scene with only a camera and a light. Choose File → Save Scene from the main menu, and Unity will prompt you for a filename for saving your scene. Save the scene in the file *360Viewer.unity*.

Import the panoramic photos into the Unity project. Locate the folder *Unity Code/ spherepano* in the code sample, and drag and drop this folder into the Assets area of the Unity Project pane. You'll see an "importing assets…" progress bar, then the folder will show up there, with thumbnails for each of the four images.

About the Images in This Chapter

The photos in this chapter were taken by Jason Marsh, super-programmer and sometimes photographer. They are free to use in any noncommercial or commercial project, with attribution: "Panoramic photos by Jason Marsh, used by permission, copyright 2015." Additional information about Jason can be found at Marsh-Works.com (*http://marshworks.com*).

You may notice that these photos are not perfectly stitched or seamlessly blended. But they are a good example of what can be done on a Samsung Galaxy Note 4 using the "Surround Shot" mode in the built-in Camera app. For all Android devices, the Camera app will do the same thing, with a mode labeled "Photo Sphere." Both apps use an Android library to provide this feature, and they are identical in underlying functionality.

Creating a panoramic background

Now, how do we turn an equirectangular 360 panoramic image into a 360 VR panorama? The answer is a lot simpler than you may expect: we just set it as a texture map on a sphere.

First, let's create a sphere in Unity. In the Hierarchy pane, click the right mouse button. You will get a menu of objects to create. Select 3D Object → Sphere. Unity's default sphere, with a radius of 1 and a gray material, will show up at the origin. Let's scale it up to 10 units in radius. Make sure that the object named *Sphere* is selected in the Hierarchy pane; then, in the Inspector pane, find the sphere's transform component. Under that you will see the Scale property; set each of the X, Y, and Z values to 10. This gives us comfortable world-sized units to work in (a 10-meter radius).

To add the texture, we simply drag and drop it onto the sphere object. In the Project pane, open the folder *Assets/spherepano*. You will see the thumbnails for the four images. Select the image *pan0*, and drag it onto the object named *Sphere* in the Hierarchy view. You should now see the panoramic image mapped onto the sphere, as shown in the screenshot in Figure 7-3.

Now, this isn't going to look quite right yet. By default, Unity positions the camera at 0, 1, –10—that is, 1 unit above the ground plane and 10 units out of the screen. To view a panoramic image in VR, we want to position the camera at the origin, so that the sphere is equally far away no matter which way we look. So, go back to the Hierarchy pane, select *Main Camera*, and set the Position property of its transform component to 0, 0, 0. That will place the camera at the origin.

Now that we have created the panorama, added the texture map, and set the camera position to the origin, we're actually ready to try this thing out. Hit the preview button (the icon at the top of the editor window that looks like a video play button). This will launch a windowed preview of the scene on your desktop computer. The result should look like Figure 7-4.

That's not what we were expecting. Where is the panorama? Don't worry, we're going to fix this in a moment. But first, we need to talk about back-face rendering.

Rendering back faces

In modern 3D systems, all rendering takes place using a *shader*: a piece of high-level programming language code whose job it is to place every 3D vertex and paint every pixel in the 2D viewport. Unity is no exception. The Unity editor supplies a standard shader that is good enough for many purposes, such as coloring and lighting a mesh, or rendering a texture map on its surface. However, Unity also lets the developer use her own shader if the situation warrants it. This situation does.

The standard Unity shader is very smart. It performs various optimizations, including one known as *back-face culling*. Put simply, *back faces* are the faces of a triangle or polygon that aren't visible from the direction from which you are looking, such as, for example, the ones that are on the inside of a geometric solid like a sphere. Since those faces are on the inside of the object and, in most circumstances, you would never see them, the standard Unity shader ignores them for rendering (or, in graphics parlance, *culls* them). But when the camera is inside a solid looking out, as is the case for our panorama, we need a way to turn off that back-face culling.

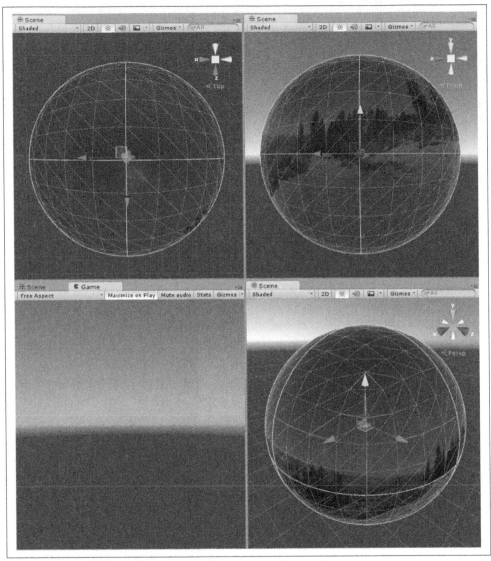

Figure 7-3. The panoramic image mapped onto a sphere

Unfortunately, the Unity standard shader does not provide a way to do this. Fortunately, some clever Unity developers have created shaders that *do* allow us to turn off back-face culling. I found one such shader via Google; it's available on the Unity developer forum (*http://bit.ly/double-sided-material*).

Figure 7-4. First preview of the 360 viewer—an empty scene, not quite right

The following listing shows the entire code for this shader, which we are going to add to our project forthwith. This source code is in the Unity shader language, which the Unity editor compiles into shader assembly code used by the machine's graphics processing unit (if you're feeling rusty, refer to Chapter 3 for a quick primer on 3D graphics concepts). Note the line in italics. By setting Cull Off, we're telling the graphics hardware to draw triangles on the "inside" of objects instead of culling them out:

```
Shader "DoubleSided" {
    Properties {
        _Color ("Main Color", Color) = (1,1,1,1)
        _MainTex ("Base (RGB)", 2D) = "white" {}
        //_BumpMap ("Bump (RGB) Illumin (A)", 2D) = "bump" {}
    }
    SubShader {
        //UsePass "Self-Illumin/VertexLit/BASE"
        //UsePass "Bumped Diffuse/PPL"

        // Ambient pass
        Pass {
        Name "BASE"
        Tags {"LightMode" = "PixelOrNone"}
        Color [_PPLAmbient]
        SetTexture [_BumpMap] {
            constantColor (.5,.5,.5)
            combine constant lerp (texture) previous
```

```
        }
    SetTexture [_MainTex] {
        constantColor [_Color]
        Combine texture * previous DOUBLE, texture*constant
        }
    }

    // Vertex lights
    Pass {
        Name "BASE"
        Tags {"LightMode" = "Vertex"}
        Material {
            Diffuse [_Color]
            Emission [_PPLAmbient]
            Shininess [_Shininess]
            Specular [_SpecColor]
            }
        SeparateSpecular On
        Lighting On
        Cull Off
        SetTexture [_BumpMap] {
            constantColor (.5,.5,.5)
            combine constant lerp (texture) previous
            }
        SetTexture [_MainTex] {
            Combine texture * previous DOUBLE, texture*primary
            }
        }
    }
    FallBack "Diffuse", 1
}
```

Let's bring this shader code into our project so that we can see our panorama. Follow this series of steps to assign the shader to the sphere mesh:

1. Locate the file *Unity Code/DoubleSided.shader* from the code sample, and drag it into *Assets* on the left side of the Project pane.

2. In the detail subpane located on the right side of the Project pane, click the right mouse button and choose Create → Material. Name it *DoubleSided*. The new material should appear in the subpane and be selected. The Inspector pane (far right) should show the properties for it.

3. Go to the Project tab again, look at the folder hierarchy in there (on the left), and single-click on the folder *Assets/spherepano*. Now, drag the image *pan0* from the Assets subpane (on the right) of the Project tab to the Base (RGB) texture preview area of the *DoubleSided* material visible in the Inspector.

4. Finally, go back to the Assets subpane of the Project tab, select the *DoubleSided* material with your mouse, and drag it onto the *Sphere* object in the Hierarchy view.

If all that went off without a hitch, you should see an immediate change reflected in the Unity editor: the Game view, located at the bottom left of the four-view layout, will now show a preview of the panorama image. See Figure 7-5, and compare that to Figure 7-3, where the bottom-left preview image showed only the generic Unity sky-box background instead of our panorama image. This is a good sign: our back faces are being rendered.

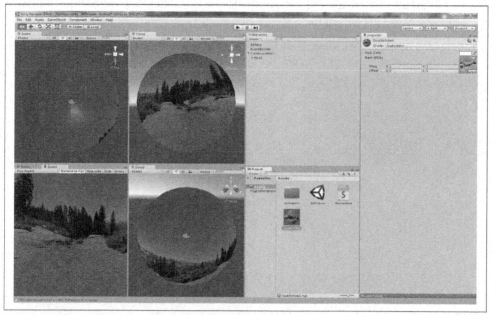

Figure 7-5. Unity scene preview showing panorama sphere with back-face rendering

Let's run one more preview to make sure we're good to go. Hit the preview button (at the top of the Unity editor window; it looks like a play button). The desktop preview window should look like the image in Figure 7-6. Now that's more like it!

Adding Cardboard VR Support

So far we haven't been worried about setting up for Cardboard VR or building for Android. We wanted to make sure we had a working 3D panorama, and as you saw, there was a bit of craft involved in getting that right. Now, we can move on to the main event. Let's get the scene rendering for Cardboard and running on a phone.

To Cardboard-enable the application, we need to import the Cardboard SDK into our Unity project, using the following steps:

1. Find the Assets pane of the Project tab in the Unity IDE. Choose Assets → Import Package → Custom Package.

2. You should see a file dialog box. Use it to navigate to the location of the downloaded Unity SDK.

3. Select the file *CardboardSDKForUnity.unitypackage*. If you downloaded the file by cloning the GitHub repo, you will find this file in the root directory.

4. Once you have clicked Open, Unity will scan the file and present you with a list of package contents to import. Just bring them all into the project: make sure that all of the objects in the list are checked, and click the Import button. You will now see assets present in the Assets pane, where there were none before.

Figure 7-6. Desktop preview of panorama viewer with back-face rendering

Now we can add the Cardboard stereo rendering and head-tracking controller to our scene. Find the prefab named *CardboardMain:* in the Project pane, select the folder *Assets/Cardboard/Prefabs*. You will see icons for each of the prefabs in the detail subpane to the right. Drag and drop *CardboardMain* from that pane into the Hierarchy pane. This will add the prefab to the scene.

Preview the scene on your desktop. It should look like the screenshot in Figure 7-7.

That's a good thing. We just want to make sure nothing's broken. Now it's time to look at it on the phone. Recall how to set up an Android build:

1. Open the Build Settings dialog by selecting File → Build Settings from the Unity main menu.

2. Select Android in the list of platforms at the bottom left, then click the Switch Platform button.

3. Add the scene to your build. The Scenes In Build list at the top will be empty to start; you need to add the current scene. Click the Add Current button, and the scene will be added to the list. You will see a checked item named *360Viewer.unity*.

4. Click the Player Settings button on the bottom left. This will open the Inspector to the Player Settings panel. (You should see it on the far right of the Unity interface.) Find the Bundle Identifier setting, and change its value to a reasonable Android package name. Make sure to change it from the default value, or Unity will complain during the build step. I used the value *vr.cardboard.Viewer360*. (Note that we need to put the *360* at the end of the bundle identifier because Android doesn't accept leading numeric characters in those strings.)

5. Finally, go back to the Build Settings dialog, plug in your phone, and click the Build And Run button. You will be prompted for a filename under which to save the *.apk* (Android package) file. I chose the name *360Viewer.apk*. That's the name that will show up on the phone in your list of apps. Hit Save to save the *.apk*.

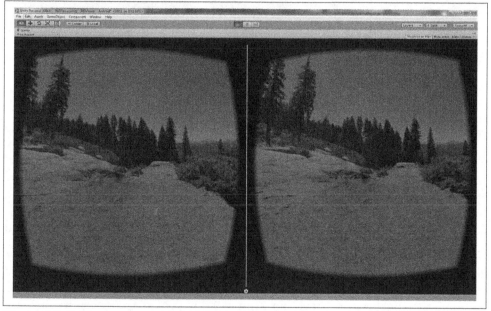

Figure 7-7. Desktop preview of Android build

If all went well, Unity will push the Android package to the phone and launch the app. Pop your phone into your Cardboard viewer, try it out, and take a look around: your first 3D panorama! Figure 7-8 shows a screenshot of the work-in-progress version.

Figure 7-8. Android screenshot of work-in-progress 360 panorama viewer

We have a few small tweaks to make. Did you notice that the image on the panorama is reversed? If you didn't, run the app again and have a look at Half Dome, which in real life faces to the left, not the right. Remember that our panorama object is a sphere with the image texture-mapped onto it. As it turns out, Unity maps the image to the *outside* of a sphere, since that's the way people typically look at them. We were able to see the sphere from inside by rigging up a double-sided shader, but that only allowed us to see the back faces; it didn't reverse the orientation of the texture. Thankfully, we can correct for this with a cheap hack: flipping the Z values on the sphere by applying a negative scale. Select the *Sphere* object in the Hierarchy pane. Then, in the Inspector pane, find the sphere's transform component. Under that you will see the Scale property; set the value of Z to −10. Build and run the app again, and you should see the panorama orientated correctly.

Now for a little cleanup. You may have seen some dark areas and flickering when looking around the panorama in the Cardboard viewer. That is because of lighting. We don't need lights in this scene, but Unity put one in by default when we first created the project. Find the object named *Directional Light* in the Hierarchy pane, and delete it (click on it with right mouse button and select Delete). While we're at it, we also don't need the default camera that came with the scene. Delete the object named *Main Camera*.

Try looking at another photo in the viewer. Replace the image on the sphere by selecting the thumbnail for *pan2* under *Assets/spherepano* in the Project pane and dragging it onto the sphere in the Hierarchy pane. Run a desktop preview to make sure it's working, then click Build And Run to try it out. You should see the new panorama:

Half Dome from within Yosemite Valley. You should also see a new material called *pan2* in the *Assets/spherepano/Materials* folder. Unity created that for you automatically when you dragged the image for *pan2* onto the sphere. It will also have the *DoubleSided* shader already set as the Shader property of the new material, because Unity remembers that setting as a sticky one from working with the previous material.

Well, that's cool. We can use our 360 viewer to experience multiple panoramas. But of course, nobody is going to do this by switching photos in the editor and rebuilding all the time—so let's make a user interface for switching them within the app.

Creating a Gaze-and-Tap User Interface

If you've been playing with virtual reality for a while, you'll be quite familiar with the gaze-and-tap interface. The VR scene contains floating objects, essentially 3D icons, that highlight when you look at them (say, by getting bigger or brighter), and trigger an action when you touch the screen, click the mouse, or interact in some other way.

For Cardboard, the popular input methods are the classic magnet switch or a similar touch switch such as DODOcase's "Popsicle stick" universal input interface, which actually generates an Android touch event by bending a piece of capacitive plastic until it touches the surface of the phone's screen, emulating the touch of your finger. For our purposes, we will assume you have a Cardboard model with the magnet switch. We are going to build a simple user interface with four square, semitransparent icons located in the bottom third of the view. When you gaze at an icon, it turns fully opaque, "selecting" the corresponding image. Pulling down on the magnet switch activates that icon, switching the panorama you are viewing.

Before we get into building the UI, let's do a little cleanup. In the Project pane, locate the material named *pan0* under *Assets/spherepano/Materials*. (Careful: make sure you are selecting the *material* and not the image of that name. Materials are represented in the Unity user interface with a square icon that contains a circle with the material rendered in a preview.) Select that material, and then click on its name beneath it. That allows you to edit the name. Rename the material to *PanoMaterial*. This is going to be the name for the material on the sphere for the panorama. We are about to create four materials, one for each of the UI icons; what we are doing now is a little materials management before we start making more stuff. While you are in there, also delete the material named *pan1*. This was created when you dropped the second pano image onto the sphere in the last step of the previous section (to view Half Dome from the floor of Yosemite Valley).

Creating a 2D Plane

For our 3D icons, we are going to use flat, square objects. We will start by making a single one, getting the properties right, and adding event handling to it. Once we have one sorted out, we will clone that to make the entire set of icons.

In the Hierarchy pane, press the right mouse button and select 3D Object → Plane. This drops a square object into the scene, oriented horizontally. Rename this object to *PanoItem0*. We want the object facing the user, not lying flat, so set the Rotation property of its transform component to 90, 180, 0. This rotates it around the *x*-axis so that it is oriented vertically, not horizontally; it also flips it about its *y*-axis so that it faces toward us, not away from us. Also, scale the object to a reasonable size, setting the Scale property to .05, .05, .05, and set the Position to 0, 0, 2, which puts the icon 2 units back along the *z*-axis. Leave it centered in *x* and *y* for now so that we are looking at it head-on; this will help us test the gaze input a few steps from now.

Now, we need to set up the material. Make sure *PanoItem0* is selected in the Hierarchy pane. Grab the texture *pan1* from the assets in the Project pane, and drag it onto *PanoItem0*. You should see the Glacier Point panorama texture on the plane. Now, we want to set up transparency on the image. Make sure the material component of *PanoItem0* shows the name *pan1*, and make sure that its Shader property is set to *Standard* in the pull-down (it was probably set to *DoubleSided* because Unity likes to remember values for things like shaders).

Expand the material properties in the Inspector by clicking the little right arrow icon next to the material's name. In the section Main Maps you will see several properties for texture map values. By the Albedo property, you should see a thumbnail of the second panorama image. To the right of that, you will see a colored rectangle, representing the material's current color. Double-click that to launch the material's color picker interface. Use that to set the alpha value of the color: enter 128 into the A input field (for 50% alpha opacity), just to the right of the slider bar for the alpha value. Then, go back to the Inspector pane and find the material's Rendering Mode property. Set that to *Transparent* in the pull-down.

If all this went according to plan, when you hit the preview button you should see a scene like the image in Figure 7-9, with the semitransparent square icon of the second panorama image dead center in the view. We now have our first icon.

Adding Input Support to the Project

In order to handle input from the magnet switch, we need to add a few more objects and components to the scene. When we are done with this part, we will have a setup similar to the gaze handling we toured in Chapter 6. Refer back to that chapter if you want to refresh your memory, or just follow the step-by-step instructions here.

Figure 7-9. Beginning icon design for the 360 viewer

First, we are going to add an object to incorporate the Cardboard SDK's input event handling. This object won't have any visual representation in the scene; it is included in the scene so that Unity's engine will continually update it each frame. Do the following:

1. In the Hierarchy pane, click the right mouse button and select Create Empty. This creates an empty Unity game object. Rename it to *EventSystem*. Now select it, and go to the Inspector pane. We are going to add a component.

2. Click the Add Component button, and from the menu that pops up, select Event → Event System. This component enables the Unity event system in your application, which supports all kinds of events in desktop and mobile environments, such as mouse up, down, click, and drag and drop. In the Inspector you will see a set of properties listed for a new component called *Event System (Script)*.

3. Click Add Component again. Choose Scripts → Gaze Input Module from the menu. This brings in the Cardboard SDK's gaze tracking system, which, among other things, determines when the user's gaze passes over an object and simulates pointer enter/exit events (i.e., mouse over/out).

4. Click Add Component one more time. Select Event → Touch Input Module. This module translates magnet switch activation into mouse clicks, delivering a pointer click event to the application.

5. We need to set up one more piece of plumbing to get our input events. The Unity engine won't pick objects unless we enable the camera to *ray cast*—that is, check

for the intersection of a ray shooting out from the camera along the current viewing direction with any objects. To enable ray casting, select the main camera by opening CardboardMain → Head → Main Camera in the Hierarchy view. Click the Add Component button, and select Event → Physics Raycaster from the pop-up menu.

Now we are ready to receive gaze over, out, and touch events. But we need to do something with them. Let's create a script to handle events.

Creating an Event Handler Script

The code samples on GitHub come with a ready-to-go event handler script. Locate the samples, find the C# source file *Unity Code/PanoItem.cs*, and drag and drop it into the Project pane's *Assets* folder. This imports the C# script into the project.

Here is how to connect the gaze and tap events set up in the previous section to our script. Select *PanoItem0* in the Hierarchy pane, and then locate its properties in the Inspector pane. Hit the Add Component button, and select Script → PanoItem from the menu that pops up. This adds a copy of the script as a component of our icon object. You should see it show up as a component named *PanoItem (Script)*. This simply adds the script to the object so that it gets updates; it doesn't connect input actions to the script yet.

To wire up event handling, add another component, this time selecting Event → Event Trigger. This is where the magic happens. You will see a new component labeled *Event Trigger (Script)*. Within that component's properties, there is a button labeled Add New Event Type. Click it and select *PointerEnter* from the pop-up menu. Then click the + icon on the small tab on the bottom right of that pane. This adds a new handler.

Now we need to associate this whole thing with a target visual object. Drag *PanoItem0* from the Hierarchy pane into the object field (where it says *None (Object)* on the left, just below the value Runtime Only). Click on the righthand combo box and select *PanoItem.SetGazedAt*. Click the checkbox right beneath that, which causes the Boolean value `true` to be passed to the script's `SetGazedAt()` method. We are going to look at the code momentarily to see what this all means; for now, let's keep connecting events and properties.

Next, add the pointer exit event. Click Add New Event Type and select *PointerExit* from the pop-up menu. Once again, Unity is good at remembering values, so *PanoItem0* should already be set up as the object. (If not, grab it in the Hierarchy pane and drag it to the object property, as we did for the *PointerEnter* event.) Click on the righthand combo box, and choose *PanoItem.SetGazedAt*. Do *not* click the checkbox right beneath it, and uncheck it if it is checked. We want `SetGazedAt()` to be called with a value of `false` on pointer exit.

The net result of all this is that when the user's gaze is over an object, the Cardboard SDK simulates a *PointerEnter* event; Unity sends it to the script for this particular icon, and then dispatches the event by calling the method `SetGazedAt(true)`. When the gaze is then not over the object, the Cardboard SDK simulates a *PointerExit* event; Unity sends it to the script for this icon, and then dispatches the event by calling the method `SetGazedAt(false)`. Do a desktop preview of the scene; you should see the icon in a highlighted state (i.e., rendered fully opaque). This is because we positioned the icon at dead center of the scene, so it is being gazed at as soon as the app launches in the preview window. The gaze handling changes the material's alpha (A) value from 50% opacity (the 128 value we entered when we first created the icon) to 100% opacity. It's time to look at the script code to see how this works.

In the Hierarchy pane, select *PanoItem0*. Now, in the Inspector, find the script component labeled *PanoItem (Script)*, which we added after we imported the script code into the project. Double-click the value to the right of the Script property label (it should say *PanoItem*, which is the name of the C# script). This will launch Unity's code editor, MonoDevelop, to view the C# source file *PanoItem.cs*. The following code listing shows a portion of this file. The lines in italics define the method `SetGazedAt()`:

```
using UnityEngine;
using System.Collections;

[RequireComponent(typeof(Collider))]
public class PanoItem : MonoBehaviour {

    public GameObject pano = null;

    // Use this for initialization
    void Start () {

        SetGazedAt(false);
    }

    // Update is called once per frame
    void Update () {

    }

    public void SetGazedAt(bool gazedAt) {
        // Debug.Log("in SetGazedAt " + (gazedAt ? "true" : "false"));

        Renderer renderer = GetComponent<Renderer>();
        Color color = renderer.material.color;
        color.a = gazedAt ? 1f : 0.5f;

        renderer.material.color = color;

    }
```

```
        . . .
    }
```

Remember, `SetGazedAt()` is called when the user looks at the icon or looks away, by the Cardboard SDK simulating pointer enter and pointer exit events that we have connected to this method. It's pretty simple: it fetches the color of the object's current material, changes its alpha value based on whether the parameter `gazedAt` is `true` or `false`, and then sets the new color value for the material. And there is it: cheap, quick and dirty, gaze-based object highlighting.

Handling Magnet Switch Events

Now let's wire up the magnet switch so that the panorama changes to a new image when the icon is tapped. The key is for the event handler script to be able to access the sphere object and update the texture map on its material, to match the texture map you are seeing in the icon.

The *PanoItem* script declares a C# class member named `pano`. This is of type `GameObject`, the base type of all Unity objects in the scene. Here is the declaration:

```
public class PanoItem : MonoBehaviour {

    public GameObject pano = null;

    // Use this for initialization
    . . .
```

If you open up the Inspector up to look at the properties for *PanoItem0*, you can see this property reflected in the Unity editor user interface. In the section for the component *PanoItem (Script)*, you will see the property name Pano. It currently has an empty value. We are going to set this value to be the sphere object as follows: drag the object *Sphere* from the Hierarchy pane and drop it onto this empty field. This will set the value of the Pano property, essentially giving the script a target object to work with. In the script code itself we will set the sphere's texture to a new value based on the texture in the specific icon item.

We also need to add the event trigger. In the Hierarchy pane, make sure *PanoItem0* is selected. Back in the Inspector pane, find the component labeled *Event Trigger (Script)*. Click the Add New Event Type button and select *PointerClick* from the pop-up menu. Click on the righthand combo box and select *PanoItem.OnClick*. This will tell the Unity event system to call the script's `OnClick()` method when the magnet switch is tapped (recall that the Cardboard framework will simulate a mouse click on a object based on the magnet switch event and the object that is being gazed at). We now have a fully wired up icon that can highlight/unlight based on gaze and change the panorama based on tap.

Here is the code for the new method, OnClick():

```
public void OnClick() {
    /*
    Debug.Log("in onClick");
    */

    Renderer renderer = GetComponent<Renderer>();

    var panoRenderer = pano.GetComponent<Renderer>();
    Texture tex = renderer.materials[0].GetTexture("_MainTex");
    panoRenderer.materials[0].SetTexture("_MainTex", tex);
}

...
```

The code to handle the tap is also really simple. It accesses the texture map stored in the first material in its list of materials (Unity rendered objects can have more than one); it uses the material's GetTexture() method to get its main texture map (Unity materials can have multiple textures); and then it sets the new value of the texture on the sphere panorama's first material. (Remember that we set our class member pano to the sphere object in the previous step.)

Ready to try it out? Hit the preview button to view the scene on the desktop. Click your mouse. If you got everything wired up correctly, you will see the panorama change to the second image. At this point, you probably can't wait to try it out on your phone. Plug it in, open File → Build Settings, and hit the Build And Run button. When the app launches on your phone, pop it into your Cardboard viewer. Pull down on the magnet switch, and the panorama will change. Success!

Creating the Functioning User Interface

There's only one more thing to do: make the full user interface. Now that we've put together a working icon, we're going to copy it to make three more. Do the following:

1. Select *PanoItem0* in the Hierarchy pane. Go to the Inspector pane and set its Position to −1.2, −1, 2. You should see it positioned on the bottom left of the scene (look at the Game view on the bottom left of the four-view layout).
2. Back in the Hierarchy pane, select *PanoItem0*, then press your right mouse button and choose Copy. Click the right mouse button again and choose Paste. A new item named *PanoItem0 (1)* will show up in the hierarchy view at the top. Rename this object to *PanoItem1*. Repeat this step two more times, creating objects named *PanoItem2* and *PanoItem3*. Now, reposition each of these objects by setting their Position properties as follows:

   - *PanoItem0*: -1.2, -1, 2
   - *PanoItem1*: -0.4, -1, 2

- *PanoItem2*: 0.4, -1>, 2
- *PanoItem3*: 1.2, -1, 2

In the Game preview you should now see the four icons laid out across the bottom of the scene.

Now we need to change the textures on the icons so that they aren't all the same image. We do that by going to the Project pane and opening the folder *Assets/sphere-pano*. We can see thumbnails for each of the textures. One by one, drag these onto the corresponding objects in the Hierarchy pane (i.e., drag *pan0* onto *PanoItem0*, *pan1* onto *PanoItem1*, *pan2* onto *PanoItem2*, and *pan3* onto *PanoItem3*). You should see the updated textures in the Game preview.

There is one last step. Because you dragged new textures onto each object, Unity created new materials for you automatically. You need to set the shader, alpha value, and rendering mode for each of the materials. Go back and select the first one, and find its material component in the Inspector. Make sure that the Shader is set to *Standard*, set the alpha value to 128 by double-clicking the color thumbnail next to Albedo and entering 128 into the A field of the color picker pop-up, and set the Rendering Mode to *Transparent*. Then do the same for the other materials.

At last, it's time to try it out. Plug your phone into the computer, choose File → Build Settings from the main menu, and click the Build And Run button. After Unity loads the Android package onto your phone, it should start the app. Place the phone into your Cardboard viewer, and take it for a spin. Gaze on each icon, pull down the magnet switch, and enjoy each 360 panorama photo. Congratulations: you've just built your first working virtual reality application!

Where to Take the Project from Here

Obviously, our little 360 photo viewer isn't going to win any awards for user interface design. This was intended as a teaching tool, to get us through the entire process of setting up a scene in Unity, dealing with the intricacies of rendering objects inside out, bringing in the Cardboard SDK for Unity, and many other nuts-and-bolts issues.

To build something you want to write home about, you might think about refining the user interface in several ways, such as using spherical icons instead of squares, or playing with different material values instead of opacity, such as color and lighting. Or you may want to play with scale, making objects slightly larger when they highlight; you could even add animated transitions between these states. You could also try laying the icons out in a cylindrical "carousel" arrangement instead of lining them up in a straight line, which would make them all appear at the same distance from the camera.

Another area for improvement would be to enable the icons to autoselect based on timeout. With this approach, when you gaze over an icon, you see a small animated cursor representing a clock. When the clock counts down to zero, the new panorama is selected. This is a great interface for Cardboard viewers that don't include a magnet or stick input switch, and we see it a lot in the current crop of Cardboard apps and demos.

Unity makes it easy to do all of these things, but you can probably already tell there are a lot of steps involved. We're almost out of time here, but feel free to strike out on your own and see what you can make, starting with the code from this project.

If you're thinking about deploying a 360 viewer for other platforms, you can use Unity to create a native desktop application, using Unity's built-in VR support for the Oculus Rift and following the build steps from Chapter 3. If, instead, you are thinking about creating a web client, have a look at Chapter 5 again. Instead of the Unity editor and the C# language, you will be in the world of a text editor like Sublime Text, a 3D framework such as Three.js, and JavaScript. This is a much cruder workflow, but by going this route, you get a few key benefits: you can deploy the application as a web page for mobile browsers, with no need for an app install, and it's easy for your application to grab panorama images from anywhere on the Web, using an HTML programming stack. Bjørn Sandvik's blog post (*http://bit.ly/photospheres-threejs*) has great information to get you going if you want to pursue creating a browser-based panorama viewer. Combine this info with the information in Chapter 5, and you'll be off and running.

Finally, if you are curious about viewing 360 videos instead of just static panoramas, you could use this project as a starting point for that. One note of caution here is that playing videos on objects in Unity currently only works in the native desktop engine; the Unity `MovieTexture` package is not available for Android. There are third-party video texture solutions for Android available on the Unity Asset Store, but as of this writing they all come with a licensing fee and no source code. Check these out at *http://bit.ly/android-movie*.

I look forward to seeing what you can come up with, from these humble beginnings.

Chapter Summary

You've finally done it: created a working virtual reality application. In this chapter we built a Cardboard VR 360-degree panoramic photo viewer, bringing together the techniques and knowledge from the previous chapters. Along the way, we reviewed core concepts, including creating 3D scenes, using the Unity3D engine and editor, using the Cardboard SDK for Unity, creating a gaze-and-tap interface, and building an application for Android.

Unity made most of our development smooth and easy, but we had to take in a lot of new information to make the application work. We learned about back-face rendering, employing a custom double-sided shader so that we could see the panorama sphere rendered from the inside. We gained insight into Unity's event system, which allows us to route input events from the mouse to objects in the application. We used the Cardboard SDK to transmute gaze and magnet switch input into the more traditional mouse-based pointer enter, pointer exit, and pointer click events. And we created a custom script in the C# language to handle the gaze and tap events to change the panorama.

Our example application, though contrived, illustrated all the basic tasks needed to build an end-to-end solution. From here, we could take it in several directions. We could refine the user interface using color, animation, and different layouts. We could target other platforms, such as the Oculus Rift. Or we could deploy a 360 viewer in a mobile browser using JavaScript. We could even adapt the photo viewer to play 360 videos, with the addition of third-party components. The possibilities are many, and very exciting.

Resources

This appendix contains lists of resources for learning more about virtual reality systems and programming tools, and VR in general.

Headsets, Input Devices, and Video Capture Systems

Headsets

High-end head-mounted displays for desktops and consoles

Several manufacturers are creating HMDs that work with desktop computers and game consoles. These include:

- The Oculus Rift (*https://www.oculus.com*)
- The HTC Vive (*http://www.htcvr.com*)
- OSVR HMDs based on the OSVR open specification (*http://sensics.com*, *http://bit.ly/osvr-hacker-dev*)
- Sony's Project Morpheus (*http://bit.ly/sony-proj-morpheus*)
- The FOVE eye-tracking HMD (*http://www.getfove.com*)

Mobile HMDs

Mobile virtual reality allows you to use the smartphone already in your pocket to experience VR, by simply dropping it into a stereoscopic viewer. Here are some of the options currently on the market:

- The Gear VR for Samsung smartphones (*http://bit.ly/samsung-gearvr*)
- Google Cardboard (list of approved headset manufacturers: *http://bit.ly/get-cardboard*)

- The Durovis Dive (*http://www.durovis.com*)
- MergeVR's Merge Goggles (*http://mergevr.com*)
- The Wearality Sky (*http://wearality.com*)

Input Devices

Input poses new challenges to design and human factors. Since the user is visually cut off from the outside world, the mouse and keyboard don't work well as input devices. Many VR applications are being designed to work with existing popular game controllers, such as those for the Xbox 360, Xbox One, or PS4, but new types of input devices and systems are also being explored. Here are some of the more promising offerings:

- Leap Motion (*https://www.leapmotion.com*)
- The Sixense STEM System (*http://sixense.com*)
- The Oculus Touch (*https://www.oculus.com*)
- The Vive hand controller (*http://www.htcvr.com*)
- The MergeVR controller (*http://mergevr.com*)

360 Video

Not all VR is created using software engines. A whole class of virtual reality experience is being developed based on 360-degree video—panoramic movies in which you are immersed and can look around without restriction. The 360 videos can be based on computer graphics animation, or they can be captured from real life using special cameras. Several companies are developing combination hardware and software systems to capture and stitch mono and stereo 360 video. If you're interested in video applications, check out the following:

- Jaunt (*http://bit.ly/jaunt-vr*) creates camera systems, stitching software, and original film productions.
- Google is developing Jump (*http://bit.ly/cardboard-jump*), a capture setup for creating 360 videos for Cardboard. The Jump rig holds 16 GoPro HERO4 cameras arranged in a circular array.
- 360Heros (*http://www.360heros.com*) creates camera rigs, production software and a 360 player, and offers production services to makers of 360 videos.
- On the low end, the RICOH THETA (*https://theta360.com/en*) is a small, handheld consumer-grade camera for capturing still and live motion 360 video.
- Kolor (*http://www.kolor.com*) develops 360 video stitching and playback software.

Applications and Content

Flagship Experiences

The following list represents just a handful of the amazing VR experiences and applications being developed:

- *EVE: Valkyrie* (*https://www.evevalkyrie.com*) is a VR multiplayer dogfighting shooter game set in the popular EVE universe: you command a heavily armed fighter in "the most realistic dogfighting game available on any platform."
- *Elite: Dangerous* (*https://www.elitedangerous.com*) is a VR space adventure, trading, and combat simulator game; this is the fourth release in the highly successful *Elite* video game series.
- *TheBlu: Encounter* (*http://wevr.com*), a breathtaking underwater environment featuring a sunken ship and a giant, unbelievably realistic blue whale, was created by VR production and technology company WEVR as one of the first showcases for the HTC Vive. (Disclosure: WEVR is my current employer.)
- *Tilt Brush* (*http://www.tiltbrush.com/#intro*) for Vive is a new version of the innovative virtual reality painting and sculpting application created by San Francisco–based development team Skillman & Hackett, now working at Google. Originally designed for the Oculus Rift, the Vive version is even more amazing, making great use of the hand controllers to provide a transcendent content creation experience.
- *Henry* (*http://bit.ly/oculus-henry*) is a touching animated piece about a lonely but loveable hedgehog, created by Oculus Story Studio, the company's in-house production team. The Story Studio is dedicated to moving VR forward as a new interactive storytelling medium.
- *The Fifth Sleep* (*http://bit.ly/fifth-sleep*) for Gear VR is a voyage through the human body and mind. Creators InnerspaceVR tell stories using animated 360-degree video developed using state-of-the-art production techniques and video game tools such as Unreal Engine and CRYENGINE.
- *Senza Peso* (*http://bit.ly/senza-peso*) is one of the original breakout cinematic VR experiences, developed for the Oculus Rift in 2014 by LA-based studio Kite and Lightning.

Noteworthy Companies

Here are a few other companies of note, not mentioned elsewhere in this appendix:

- VRSE (*http://vrse.com*) is a production company telling stories in VR, founded by noted experimental filmmaker Chris Milk.

- Vantage.tv (*http://vantage.tv*) captures live events such as concerts and music festivals. You can experience the events online using their player and even share in the fun in real time with up to four friends.
- NextVR (*http://www.nextvr.com*) delivers live and on-demand virtual reality experiences in broadcast quality.

Download Sites

Many great VR apps and experiences are available for download, hosted by Oculus, Valve, and others. Here are a few sites to get you started:

- Oculus Share (*https://share.oculus.com*)
- SteamVR (*http://bit.ly/streamvr*)

WebVR Showcases and Applications

I am firm believer that the Web holds one of the keys to virtual reality's future. While the technology of WebVR is still on the bleeding edge, and trailing behind on performance (ever so slightly), development proceeds apace and there are already some really cool showcase experiences. For example:

- Mozilla's WebVR showcase site, MozVR (*http://mozvr.com*), offers demos, downloads, and a blog providing tips for developers and reporting on current projects.
- Chrome Experiments (*https://vr.chromeexperiments.com*) for VR is a site that features demos for Google Cardboard written completely with mobile browser technology.
- Vizor (*http://vizor.io*) is a browser-based content creation and cloud hosting platform for WebVR.
- WebVR 360 video players are being developed by EleVR (*http://elevr.com*) and LittlStar (*http://littlstar.com*).

SDKs, Development Tools, and Programming Languages

Device SDKs

The VR development stack runs the gamut of software SDKs, tools, programming languages, and frameworks. Depending on what device you're targeting, here are some of the SDKs you're likely to need:

- Oculus (*http://developer.oculus.com*) provides SDKs for developing for the Rift on the desktop and for the Gear VR for Samsung smartphones.

- OpenVR (*http://bit.ly/open-vr*) is a C++ API and runtime developed by Valve that allows access to VR hardware from multiple vendors, without requiring that applications have specific knowledge of the hardware they are targeting. It is currently being used to develop applications for the HTC Vive. It also comes with Unity and Unreal plugin packages.
- OSVR (*https://github.com/OSVR*), not to be confused with OpenVR, is an open source software platform for virtual and augmented reality applications. It allows discovery, configuration, and operation of a range of VR devices on a variety of platforms and supports many types of devices, from HMDs to trackers and more. OSVR is being developed by a close consortium of companies including VR developers Sensics and peripheral maker Razer.
- Google (*http://bit.ly/cardboard-dev*) provides both native Android (Java) and Unity SDKs for Cardboard.

Game Engine Middleware

Today, most virtual reality is developed using game engines and associated editing and pipeline tools, known collectively as *middleware*. Here are some of the most popular options:

- Unity3D (*http://unity3d.com*) is the indie game development tool of choice, featured heavily in this book.
- Unreal Engine (*http://bit.ly/unreal-engine-4*), created by powerhouse game developer Epic Games, is feature rich and growing in popularity for VR development.
- CRYENGINE (*http://cryengine.com*) is another powerful engine created by successful developer Crytek.

Programming Languages

The book covered several development languages. If you're unfamiliar with one or more of these languages, start with the Wikipedia entries for a history and then search online using your favorite search engine:

- Originally created by Microsoft for its .NET framework, C# (*http://bit.ly/wiki-csharp*) was chosen by Unity as its preferred language for developing scripts. An investment in learning C# will get you going with Unity, which targets the most platforms and VR systems of any game development tool today.
- An old horse in early web and enterprise server development, Java (*http://bit.ly/wiki-java*) got new life when it became the main programming language for the Android mobile operating system. The Google Cardboard native SDK and the GearVRf framework from Samsung (see the next section) are written in Java.
- JavaScript (*http://bit.ly/wiki-js*) is the scripting language for web browsers. It has grown from humble beginnings as a "toy" scripting language into a powerful lan-

guage used by millions of developers, from hobbyists to professional engineers. It is arguably the most widely used programming language on the planet. JavaScript is the language you want to use if you are looking at developing web-based VR applications, either for the newer WebVR API or for Cardboard-style rendering and head tracking.

Software Frameworks

In addition to the game engine middleware listed earlier, there are other software frameworks available for programming VR. These frameworks are code only, not packaged with an editor like Unity or Unreal. Some examples are:

- GearVRf (*http://gearvrf.org*) is a native Java framework for creating VR applications, developed by Samsung. GearVRf is fully open source with no license restrictions.
- WebVR is an open effort that includes specifications, software implementations (browsers), a mailing list for discussion, and JavaScript frameworks for coding. The WebVR specifications can be found at *http://bit.ly/webvr-spec*. The WebVR mailing list is at *web-vr-discuss@mozilla.org*.
- Firefox Nightly builds for desktop and Android are available at *https://nightly.mozilla.org*.
- Chromium development builds and mobile betas can be found at *http://bit.ly/chromium-webvr-builds* and *http://bit.ly/chromium-webview*.
- WebVR programming frameworks use WebGL for in-browser rendering and the WebVR APIs for head tracking and fullscreen stereo rendering. They include:
  — Three.js (*http://threejs.org*)
  — Babylon.js (*http://www.babylonjs.com*)
  — SceneJS (*http://scenejs.org*)
  — GLAM (*http://glamjs.org*)
- WebVR 360 video player engines include open source projects from eleVR (*http://bit.ly/elebr-web-player*) and Littlstar (*https://github.com/littlstar*).

Websites

There are a growing number of news sites, blogs, and podcasts devoted to virtual reality. Here is a selection of some of the best:

- Upload VR (*http://uploadvr.com*)
- Road to VR (*http://www.roadtovr.com*)
- Voices of VR (*http://voicesofvr.com*)
- Enter VR (*http://entervr.net*)

Meetup Groups

Meetup groups are a vital resource for learning about VR and networking with like-minded developers, artists, and thinkers. The San Francisco Bay Area alone plays host to more than a dozen VR-related meetup groups, including:

- Silicon Valley Virtual Reality (*http://bit.ly/sv-vr-meetup*), the original VR meetup group, always exploring the latest in virtual reality development.
- San Francisco Virtual Reality (*http://www.meetup.com/virtualreality*), a booming meetup group with over 1,000 members, featuring great demos and speakers.
- San Francisco WebVR (*http://www.meetup.com/Web-VR*), a group devoted to WebVR development (I'm the co-organizer of this group).
- Kaleidoscope SF (*http://www.meetup.com/kaleido-SF*), a group dedicated to virtual reality filmmaking and storytelling (formerly VR Cinema).

Index

About the Author

Tony Parisi is an entrepreneur and career CTO/software architect. He has developed international standards and protocols, created noteworthy software products, and started and sold technology companies. Tony's passion for innovating is exceeded only by his desire to build great products.

Tony is a pioneer in virtual reality, the co-creator of the VRML and X3D ISO standards for networked 3D graphics, and continues to innovate in 3D technology. He is the co-organizer of the San Francisco WebGL Meetup (*http://bit.ly/sf-webgl*), and the San Francisco WebVR Meetup (*http://www.meetup.com/Web-VR/*), and a member of the Khronos COLLADA working group creating glTF (*http://www.gltf.gl/*), the new file format standard for 3D web and mobile applications. Tony is also the author of two O'Reilly books on WebGL: *WebGL: Up and Running* (2012) and *Programming 3D Applications with HTML5 and WebGL* (2014).

Tony is currently VP of Platform Products at WEVR, a virtual reality community and VR media player for aspiring and professional creatives.

Colophon

The animal on the cover of *Learning Virtual Reality* is a Salvin's prion (*Pachyptila salvini*). The species is named for the British ornithologist Osbert Salvin.

This small petrel breeds principally on the Île aux Cochons in the Crozet Islands, where four million pairs are thought to nest. Other breeding colonies include Prince Edward Island, St. Paul Island, and Amsterdam Island. At sea they range from South Africa eastwards to New Zealand.

Salvin's prion is only 11 inches long, sporting white and gray feathers and a blue bill with serrated edges that contains between seven and nine horny plates, giving the bird, in part, its name (*priōn* is Greek for "saw"). The bill is fitted with lamellae, enabling the prion to filter seawater for krill and amphipods, its main diet.

The prion produces a foul-smelling stomach oil that can be sprayed at predators as a defense mechanism. It also serves as a nutrient-rich food store for chicks and for their parents during long flights over the ocean.

Many of the animals on O'Reilly covers are endangered; all of them are important to the world. To learn more about how you can help, go to *animals.oreilly.com*.

The cover image is from *The English Cyclopaedia of Natural History*. The cover fonts are URW Typewriter and Guardian Sans. The text font is Adobe Minion Pro; the heading font is Adobe Myriad Condensed; and the code font is Dalton Maag's Ubuntu Mono.

Get even more for your money.

Join the O'Reilly Community, and register the O'Reilly books you own. It's free, and you'll get:

- $4.99 ebook upgrade offer
- 40% upgrade offer on O'Reilly print books
- Membership discounts on books and events
- Free lifetime updates to ebooks and videos
- Multiple ebook formats, DRM FREE
- Participation in the O'Reilly community
- Newsletters
- Account management
- 100% Satisfaction Guarantee

Signing up is easy:

1. Go to: oreilly.com/go/register
2. Create an O'Reilly login.
3. Provide your address.
4. Register your books.

Note: English-language books only

To order books online:
oreilly.com/store

For questions about products or an order:
orders@oreilly.com

To sign up to get topic-specific email announcements and/or news about upcoming books, conferences, special offers, and new technologies:
elists@oreilly.com

For technical questions about book content:
booktech@oreilly.com

To submit new book proposals to our editors:
proposals@oreilly.com

O'Reilly books are available in multiple DRM-free ebook formats. For more information:
oreilly.com/ebooks

CPSIA information can be obtained at www.ICGtesting.com
Printed in the USA
BVOW09s1456031115

424978BV00002B/2/P